S0-APN-908

MACLAY SCHOOL LIBRARY
3737 N. MERIDIAN ROAD
TALLAHASSEE, FL 32312

GREAT FIGURES
OF THE
WILD WEST

By Paul Robert Walker:

Pride of Puerto Rico: The Story of Roberto Clemente
A biography for young readers

The Method
A novel for young adults

Bigfoot and Other Legendary Creatures
Illustrated fiction/nonfiction

A M E R I C A N

P R O F I L E S

Great Figures
of the
Wild West

■

Paul Robert Walker

MACLAY SCHOOL LIBRARY
3737 N. MERIDIAN ROAD
TALLAHASSEE, FL 32312

Facts On File®

AN INFOBASE HOLDINGS COMPANY

Great Figures of the Wild West

Copyright © 1992 by Paul Robert Walker

All rights reserved. No part of this book may be reproduced or utilized in any form or by any means, electronic or mechanical, including photo-copying, recording, or by any information storage or retrieval systems, without permission in writing from the publisher. For information contact:

Facts On File, Inc.
460 Park Avenue South
New York NY 10016

Library of Congress Cataloging-in-Publication Data
Walker, Paul Robert.
    Great figures of the Wild West / Paul Robert Walker.
      p. cm. — (American profiles)
    Includes bibliographical references and index.
    Summary: Profiles eight people who helped shape the popular image of the Wild West: Sitting Bull, Buffalo Bill, Jesse James, Wyatt Earp, Billy the Kid, Geronimo, Belle Starr, and Judge Roy Bean.
    ISBN 0-8160-2576-2 (acid-free paper)
    1. West (U.S.)—History—1848–1950—Biography—Juvenile literature. 2. Frontier and pioneer life—West (U.S.)—Juvenile literature. [1. West (U.S.)—Biography. 2. Frontier and pioneer life.] I. Title. II. Series: American profiles (Facts On File, Inc.)
F594.W215 1992
978'.00992—dc20
[B]   91-9744

British CIP data available on request from Facts On File.

Facts On File books are available at special discounts when purchased in bulk quantities for businesses, associations, institutions or sales promotions. Please contact our Special Sales Department in New York at 212/683-2244 or 800/322-8755.

Text design by Ron Monteleone

MP FOF Printed in the United States of America

10 9 8 7 6 5 4 3 2

This book is printed on acid-free paper.

To
my mother, Elsie H. K. Walker,
a pioneer in her own right

Contents

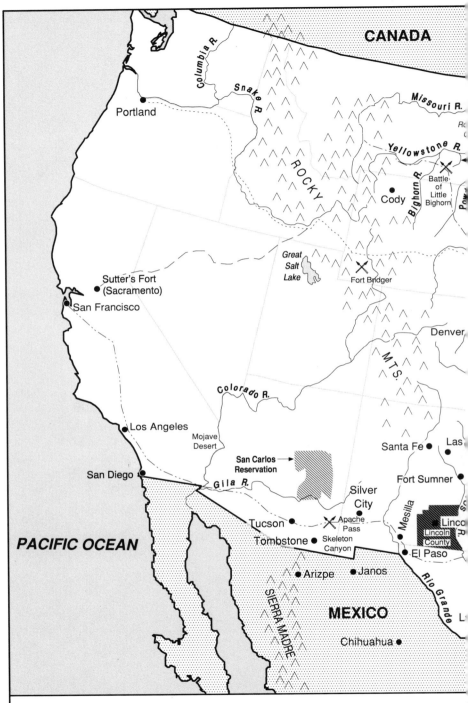

CANADA

Columbia R.

Snake R.

Missouri R.

Yellowstone R.

ROCKY

Bighorn R.

Battle of Little Bighorn

Cody

Portland

Great Salt Lake

Fort Bridger

Denver

Sutter's Fort (Sacramento)

San Francisco

MTS.

Colorado R.

Los Angeles

Santa Fe

Las

Mojave Desert

San Carlos Reservation

Fort Sumner

San Diego

Gila R.

Silver City

Mesilla

PACIFIC OCEAN

Tucson

Apache Pass

Lincoln County

Linco

Tombstone

Skeleton Canyon

El Paso

Arizpe

Janos

Rio Grande

SIERRA MADRE

MEXICO

Chihuahua

This map is designed to help the reader locate the places and geographical features mentioned in the text; it doe
include every important location in the history of the Wild West. Current state boundaries are provided for refere
Other boundaries and names reflect those in effect during the events described in this book.

CANADA

t Buford

eer
ntain

Standing
Rock
Reservation

adwood

Wounded
Knee

Fort
Randall

N. Platte

Platte R.

mit
ngs

Omaha

nd
ek
acre

Dodge
City

Wichita

L. Superior

Minneapolis

Northfield

Sioux City

Council
Bluffs

St. Joseph

Leavenworth

Kansas City

Independence

Scott
County

Corydon

Gallatin

Chicago

L. Huron

L. Erie

Clay
County

St. Louis

Carthage

Canadian R.

Indian
Territory

Fort Smith

Arkansas R.

Youngers
Bend

Fort Sill

Fort Worth

Dallas

Scyene

Red R.

Mississippi R.

New
Orleans

garoon

Austin

San Antonio
(Beanville)

Rio Grande

ICO

Gulf
of
Mexico

— — —	California Trail
··········	Oregon Trail
—·—·—	Bozeman Trail
—··—··—	Butterfield Stage Line
◼	Forts
✕	Battles
▨	Counties
▧	Indian Territories and Reservations

0   100   200 MI

0   100   200 Km

Introduction

*Deadwood, Dakota Territory, in 1876. A typical
boomtown of the Wild West, Deadwood grew
quickly after the discovery of gold in the Black Hills.*
(National Archives. Photograph by S. J. Morrow)

---

*T*he Wild West! Cowboys and Indians. Wagon trains and
stagecoaches rattling over the Plains. The blue-coated cavalry
saving the pioneers. Good guys with white hats and bad guys with
black hats. Gunslingers shooting it out on dusty streets. Saloons
with beautiful dance-hall girls and gamblers in fancy vests. Heroic
lawmen standing up to the outlaws.

If that description sounds familiar, you've been watching old movies and television shows. The real Wild West was not as simple as it is usually portrayed in westerns. Of course there were cowboys, Indians, cavalry, and the rest. But it was pretty difficult to tell the good guys from the bad guys, and true heroes were hard to find. No one worried too much about the color of his hat. In fact, the *real* good guys—the Indians fighting to preserve their culture and their land—didn't wear hats at all.

Why do we have such a simple, black-and-white picture of the Wild West? One reason is that movies and television lend themselves to simple stories. It's easier to follow the action if the good guys wear white hats and the bad guys wear black.

But movies and television did not create the image. It was established as the events occurred in the second half of the 19th century. At that time, newspaper editors and writers were often more concerned with entertaining their readers than reporting the truth. They would exaggerate a story that would then be picked up by another paper and exaggerated again. Soon a legend was born.

Mass-produced adventure stories called dime novels added to the confusion. They would often claim to tell the "true story" of a real person, such as Buffalo Bill or Jesse James. In fact, the story was usually the product of the writer's imagination from start to finish. The reader might accept the "truth," and once again a legend would be born.

In the case of the Indians, official military and government reports often obscured the truth. Most white people, including army officers and government officials, had little or no understanding of the Indians. They considered them uncivilized savages who were standing in the way of civilization. This was, of course, not true. But it added to the myth of the Wild West.

So what was the real Wild West?

First, the Wild West was a place. In general, it was the land west of the Mississippi River. More specifically, it might be defined as the area southwest of the Missouri River and east of San Francisco. The actual location changed as white civilization pushed westward. Wherever the "civilized" world met the unsettled wilderness, that was the Wild West.

Second, the Wild West was a time. In general, it was the second half of the 19th century, beginning with the California gold rush of 1849. More specifically, it was the period from the end of the Civil War in 1865 to the U.S. census of 1890. This census estab-

Introduction

lished that there was no longer a single large unsettled area in the continental United States. The historian Frederick Jackson Turner interpreted the census information as indicating the "death of the frontier."

Finally, the Wild West was a state of mind—an idea—a way of life that developed in the United States in a particular place and at a particular time. It was a tough, violent life; yet it was a life of great freedom and opportunity. Why did this idea, this kind of life, develop in this place and this time? There is no single answer, but there are a number of important reasons.

Perhaps the single most powerful force in the development of the Wild West was the Civil War. Physically, psychologically, and economically, the war ripped the nation apart. When peace finally returned, many people on both sides looked westward for a new start. This was especially true of former Confederate soldiers who faced discrimination in their home states.

Some former Confederate soldiers, such as Jesse James, became outlaws; most became law-abiding citizens. But the atmosphere of violence from the war—and the experience of using guns on a daily basis—carried over to the western settlements. The hatred between Union supporters and Confederate supporters also carried over. Many Wild West conflicts involved former Union men on one side and former Confederates on the other side.

The enormous cost of the war also contributed to the development and violence of the West. The government needed gold and silver to pay off its debts. It was eager to exploit western mining areas, regardless of earlier treaties or agreements with the Indians. In 1865 this caused an outbreak of hostilities with the Sioux, who were trying to keep miners out of their hunting grounds. The presence of American miners on Indian lands was also an important factor in the conflicts with the Apache.

Of course, the miners were not risking their lives in order to help the government. They were hoping to strike it rich. This was the next great factor in the development of the Wild West: economic opportunity. In the cities of the East, a man needed money to start a business. But in the wide open spaces of the West, all he needed was hard work and a little luck.

A miner could rise from a pauper to a prince overnight—if he could only find the mother lode. It didn't happen very often, but it *did* happen. And that was enough to bring young men streaming into the wilderness with nothing but a gold pan and a prayer. A successful mining region quickly developed a wild "boomtown," where the miners could sell their gold, buy supplies, and spend their money on gambling, drinking, and prostitutes.

It didn't take much money to be a cattle baron either. There were longhorns running wild in Texas, and the range was open to everyone. After the wild cattle were gone, a cattleman could sneak over to Mexico and steal 20 or 30 head. Or he could just sneak over to his neighbor's herd. There were no fences on the open range, and it wasn't hard to change a brand. Many Wild West battles began over stolen cattle.

There was opportunity in farming as well. The Homestead Act of 1862 offered 160 acres of free land to anyone who would claim it, live on it, and improve it. Other acts allowed settlers to claim up to 640 acres in the dry areas of the West, where more land was necessary to make a profit. There were many conflicts between farmers and ranchers over the use and protection of the land.

The directors of the Union Pacific Railroad stand beside the tracks on the 100th meridian, 247 miles west of Omaha, Nebraska Territory, in October 1866. Two and one half years later, the Union Pacific connected with the Central Pacific at Promontory, Utah, and formed the first transcontinental railroad.
(National Archives. Photograph by John Carbutt)

The third great factor in the development of the Wild West was the building of the railroads. In 1867 the Kansas Pacific Railroad reached Abilene, Kansas, providing transportation for Texas long-

Introduction

horn cattle to the markets of the East. This was the first "cow-town," where cowboys spent their hard-earned money on the same wild entertainment that miners found in the boomtowns. Lawmen such as Wyatt Earp and Wild Bill Hickok first gained fame in the Kansas cowtowns.

Between 1862 and 1871, the U.S. government gave various railroad companies a total of 174 million acres of public lands to help pay the cost of constructing transcontinental railroads. The railroads offered this land for sale, advertising throughout the United States and Europe. This program was one of the most important forces in settling the West, but, like the cowtowns and boomtowns, it brought many people into the wilderness before traditional law enforcement and other services could be developed.

The final factor that contributed to the atmosphere of the Wild West was the resistance of the American Indians. In his biography of Sitting Bull, Stanley Vestal pointed out that if the Indians did not exist, the history of the West would have been "a dull chronicle of plodding clodhoppers, placidly moving each year a little farther onto the vacant lands, carrying along their petty, European culture, unchanged and unchanging." This is perhaps an exaggeration—the rugged land itself would have forced some changes on the American pioneers. But the violent conflict between two completely different cultures was a key aspect of the Wild West.

This book includes profiles of eight people who helped shape our image of the Wild West. They are not necessarily the most important people in the history of the West. Some were very important; others were minor players on the western stage. What they all have in common is fame. A century later these eight names still represent the Wild West: Sitting Bull, Buffalo Bill, Jesse James, Wyatt Earp, Billy the Kid, Geronimo, Belle Starr, and Judge Roy Bean.

Their stories have been told many times in books, plays, movies, and television shows. But like the true story of the Wild West, their true stories have often been lost in legend. This is unfortunate because, while the legends are very entertaining, the true stories are even better. By examining the real lives of these legendary figures, we can learn more about the real Wild West.

From a historical point of view, the Indian leaders, Sitting Bull and Geronimo, are the most important figures in the book. They are also the most heroic. Although they never met and were quite different in personality, their lives were very similar. Sitting Bull was the last Sioux leader to surrender to the white man. Geronimo was the last Apache leader. They fought because they loved their people and their way of life. They lost only because there were too many white men.

The two lawmen, Wyatt Earp and Judge Roy Bean, illustrate the hazy law enforcement of the Wild West. Earp has been portrayed as a heroic marshal in countless westerns, but he was neither a hero nor a marshal. Many people viewed him as a criminal hiding behind a badge. That is probably too harsh—at least Earp provided some law and order in the wild towns of Kansas and Arizona. Judge Roy Bean was a petty criminal hiding behind a law book, but like Earp, he provided law and order where it was desperately needed.

The career of Jesse James represents the continuing conflict of the Civil War; despite his crimes he was considered a hero by many Confederate sympathizers. The criminal life of Belle Starr also developed out of the Civil War; her life is a clear reminder that women made their mark in the Wild West. Billy the Kid was too young to take part in the war, but like Jesse James, he was considered a hero by many people. In the Wild West, the difference between a hero and an outlaw often depended on your point of view.

Buffalo Bill Cody lived the real life of the Wild West as a soldier and scout, making important contributions in a number of campaigns against the Indians. He then helped to create the myth of the Wild West as an actor and a showman. Cody tried to accurately portray the life he had experienced, but his Wild West show led to many less accurate imitations. In a sense, Buffalo Bill Cody invented the western.

The Wild West was a big, unsettled land where a person could ride all day without seeing another human being. Yet there were some very interesting connections between these eight people. Sitting Bull appeared in Buffalo Bill's Wild West show, and Cody was later sent to arrest his former star attraction. Jesse James hid out with Belle Starr and apparently visited Billy the Kid. Wyatt Earp rode in a posse that unsuccessfully tried to capture Geronimo.

The eight profiles are arranged in approximate chronological order—not by year of birth, but by the period when the figure first emerged on the Wild West scene. Judge Roy Bean, born around 1825, is the oldest; yet he did not become famous until he was in his sixties. Billy the Kid, born around 1859, is the youngest, but he achieved fame by the age of 21. Billy was dead before America knew Roy Bean existed.

Bean and Billy are typical of the opportunity and violence of the Wild West. An old man could create a new life when he might have been thinking of retirement. A young man could become famous and dead before he was old enough to vote.

Sitting Bull:
The Spirit of the Sioux

*Sitting Bull wearing ceremonial headdress of
Teton Sioux chief. Taken around 1885,
several years after his surrender.*
(National Archives. Photograph by David F. Barry)

Sitting Bull stood on the shore of Sylvan Lake in the heart of the
Black Hills. A beautiful song echoed across the water, and the
young warrior searched for the singer. On top of a rock rising
above the lake was a figure that looked like a man. As Sitting Bull
climbed toward the figure, it turned around to look at him. Now
he could see that it was not a man—it was an eagle. He climbed
closer, but the eagle flew away.

The Black Hills are the sacred land of the Sioux people—a gift from Wakan Tanka, the Great Spirit. Sitting Bull knew that this was not an ordinary eagle. And it was not an ordinary song. It was a message from Wakan Tanka—a message that would control his destiny. Slowly, in his strong, beautiful voice, Sitting Bull began to sing the eagle's song:

> *My Father has given me this nation;*
> *In protecting them I have a hard time.*

This vision was the turning point in the life of Sitting Bull, the great chief of the Teton Sioux. In his biography, *Sitting Bull: Champion of the Sioux*, Stanley Vestal wrote: "Thereafter Sitting Bull believed himself 'god-chosen,' divinely appointed to lead and protect his people. This sober conviction was the driving, guiding force which sparked his whole career—a heavy responsibility which he fully accepted and carried conscientiously to his dying day."

Sitting Bull was born around March 1831 near the Grand River in what is now northwestern South Dakota. He was a member of the Hunkpapa, one of seven subtribes of the Teton Sioux. Today the Teton Sioux are often called the Lakota.

The Teton were the largest and fiercest of the Sioux tribes. They were nomadic buffalo hunters, moving their camps in search of the great beasts that provided them with food, clothing, and shelter. When Sitting Bull was born, the Teton ranged throughout the northern Plains in the area that now includes Nebraska, Wyoming, South Dakota, North Dakota, and Montana.

As a child, Sitting Bull was named Slow because of his careful, thoughtful personality. At the age of 14, Slow joined a group of warriors who were looking for an enemy tribe. When they found the other tribe, he was the first to count *coup*, striking an enemy warrior with a long stick. In the warfare of the Plains Indians, counting *coup* was the greatest honor, and the first *coup* of the battle was the greatest honor of all. Slow's father gave him a new name in honor of his bravery: *Tatanka Iyotake*, which means "Sitting Bull."

Sitting Bull grew up to be a powerful warrior. In 1856, when he was 25 years old, he killed a Crow chief in one-on-one combat. He came away from the battle with a bullet wound in his left foot—a wound that never healed properly and left him with a permanent limp. But he also came away with the respect of the other warriors. He was elected chief of a society called the Midnight Strong Hearts. These were the bravest warriors of the Hunkpapa, and they were loyal to Sitting Bull.

Until the 1860s, Sitting Bull's only contact with white men was with traders who sold him guns, ammunition, and other supplies in exchange for buffalo hides. As the most northern of the Teton subtribes, the Hunkpapa were far removed from the early conflicts with white settlers along the Oregon Trail. However, the southern Teton did encounter whites during the 1840s and 1850s, and it is likely that Sitting Bull heard stories of the thousands of white men who were crossing the Plains. The worst part of these stories was that when the whites came, their animals and wagons destroyed the grass. Then the buffalo disappeared.

In 1863 the Hunkpapa traveled east across the Missouri River to hunt buffalo. They met a band of eastern Sioux under a leader named Inkpaduta. The eastern Sioux, called Santee, had been driven out of Minnesota after a bloody battle with the whites. Although most of the Santee had surrendered, Inkpaduta's band was still fighting. The Hunkpapa joined their eastern cousins in minor skirmishes with American infantry and cavalry.

A year later, on July 28, 1864, the Hunkpapa once again camped with Inkpaduta's band at Killdeer Mountain in what is now North Dakota. Two thousand American soldiers under General Alfred Sully attacked the camp with artillery. Although the camp was destroyed, 1,600 Sioux warriors successfully protected the retreat of their women and children. Sitting Bull was not impressed with the blue-coated soldiers during these early conflicts. However, he saw the power of their big guns. There was little the Indians could do against artillery.

In the spring of 1865, a group of Cheyenne—who were friends of the Sioux—came to Sitting Bull's camp and told him a very disturbing story. A few months earlier, in November 1864, 600 American soldiers had marched into a Cheyenne village at Sand Creek, Colorado, and killed over 200 Cheyenne, mostly women and children. The Indians were friendly to the Americans and camping peacefully; it was not a battle—it was a massacre. When Sitting Bull heard about this horrible incident, his heart began to harden toward the white man.

The Sand Creek Massacre was part of a conflict that began with the discovery of gold in Colorado. It seemed that when the white

3

man wanted the yellow metal, he had no respect for the Indian lands. In 1862 gold was discovered in the mountains of Montana. The following year the Bozeman Trail was opened as the shortest route to the goldfields. The trail passed directly through the Powder River hunting grounds of the Teton Sioux. As more miners entered their territory, the Sioux began to attack the wagon trains on the trail.

In August 1865, General Patrick Connor led a large expedition into the Powder River country. Its purpose was to defeat the Sioux and Cheyenne, make the area safe for miners, and open another road to the goldfields. On September 8, 400 warriors, including Sitting Bull, attacked part of Connor's force near the mouth of the Little Powder River. For the next few days they harassed the Americans, chasing them out of the area. The expedition was a complete disaster.

Frustrated by the failure of the Powder River Expedition, the soldiers began to build a series of forts along the Bozeman Trail in 1866. This set off a period of heavy fighting called Red Cloud's War, named after the Oglala Sioux warrior who led the Indian resistance. Sitting Bull and the Hunkpapa were not involved in this fighting. They were still able to withdraw from the white man and live their traditional life on the northern Plains. But they could feel the white people coming closer and closer.

By 1868 Red Cloud had achieved his main objective of closing the forts on the Bozeman Trail. He was willing to make peace with the whites and lead his people onto a reservation—where they would live within boundaries defined by the U.S. government. However, most of the Teton Sioux wanted to keep fighting and drive the white man from their land. The Teton realized that they were facing a powerful enemy. They would have to fight together.

Traditionally, the Teton did not have a single head chief. They were very independent people, and even within a subtribe such as the Hunkpapa there were a number of chiefs, each with his own following. To unite the subtribes, they had to find a man whom everyone could respect; a man whose bravery was unquestioned but who could also think clearly and calmly; a man of spiritual power whose prayers were answered by Wakan Tanka. Around 1867 most of the Teton subtribes, as well as some of the Cheyenne, Arapaho, and eastern Sioux, decided that Sitting Bull was the one man they could all follow. Crazy Horse, an Oglala warrior who had fought with Red Cloud, was chosen second-in-command.

In June 1868, a Jesuit missionary named Father Pierre-Jean De Smet made a courageous trip to Sitting Bull's camp and convinced the hostile Sioux to try to live in peace with the whites. Two Hunkpapa leaders named Gall and Bull Owl traveled to Fort Rice in the Dakota Territory where they signed a new treaty on July 2, 1868. Red Cloud signed the treaty the following November.

The Treaty of 1868 granted the Sioux a huge reservation covering the western half of what is now the state of South Dakota, including the sacred Black Hills. This land, called the Great Sioux Reservation, was guaranteed to the Sioux forever, and no white man was allowed to enter it except for certain government employees. The Sioux were also granted hunting rights in the Powder River country. The forts on the Bozeman Trail were abandoned, and the trail itself was closed.

In order to administer the treaty, a number of government agencies were established on or near the reservation. The agents issued food and supplies to the "good" Indians who agreed to settle on the reservation. They also tried to "civilize" them by encouraging farming and educating their children. Each agent was aided by a small staff that might include a physician, a farmer, a teacher, a carpenter, and a blacksmith.

Most of the southern Teton leaders signed the Treaty of 1868, but many northern leaders, including Sitting Bull, ignored it and continued to roam over their traditional land—on and off the Great Sioux Reservation. Although Sitting Bull continued to lead war parties against his Indian enemies, he attempted to live peacefully with the whites. Or to be more accurate, he attempted to live peacefully *without* the whites. Unlike Red Cloud, he refused to become an "agency Indian," dependent on the government for food and supplies.

In 1872, 400 American soldiers escorted a surveying party that was charting the future route of the Northern Pacific Railroad directly through the Sioux hunting grounds. Sitting Bull and his warriors skirmished with the soldiers, but the surveyors returned the next summer with an even larger guard, including the Seventh Cavalry under Lieutenant Colonel George Armstrong Custer. In August 1873, Custer and several cavalry companies fought a major battle with the Sioux, Cheyenne, and Arapaho at the Yellowstone River. Although the Indians were unable to drive the whites away, the whites were also unable to defeat the Indians.

During one of these conflicts, a Sioux medicine man convinced a group of young warriors that they were immune to the white man's bullets. Upon seeing that the warriors were in fact being injured, Sitting Bull ordered them to retreat. When the medicine man questioned the chief's courage, Sitting Bull set down his weapons, walked out in front of the soldiers, and calmly smoked his pipe while bullets whizzed past him. Although this accomplished nothing from a military point of view, it convinced the warriors that there was nothing wrong with Sitting Bull's courage.

A column of cavalry, artillery, and wagons commanded by Lieutenant Colonel George Armstrong Custer during the Black Hills expedition of 1874.
(National Archives. Photograph by W. H. Illingworth)

In the summer of 1874, Custer led an expedition into the Black Hills—the sacred land that had been promised to the Sioux forever. This expedition violated the Treaty of 1868, which guaranteed that no white man would enter the Great Sioux Reservation. However the United States was in the midst of an economic depression, and there were rumors of gold in the Black Hills. Custer reported that the Black Hills were the most beautiful area he had ever seen. There were plenty of trees, plenty of water, and the soil was rich. It was perfect for farming. But even better—there was "gold among the roots of the grass."

Custer's report set off a stampede of miners heading for the Black Hills—again in direct violation of the Treaty of 1868. The army made a few halfhearted attempts to stop the flow, but it was hopeless. The American public wanted the Black Hills opened for mining. In September 1875, a meeting was held to discuss the sale of mining rights in the Black Hills. To the Indians, there was no difference between selling the mining rights and selling the land. Sitting Bull was invited to the meeting but refused to attend. "We want no white men here," he said. "The Black Hills belong to me. If the whites try to take them, I will fight."

In December 1875, the Department of Interior—which had jurisdiction over Indian affairs—issued a proclamation that all Sioux must be on the reservation before January 31, 1876. If they did not report to an agency they would be considered "hostile" and, when captured, would be turned over to the army for punishment. By the time most of the Sioux heard of this decree, it was impossible to travel through the harsh winter of the northern Plains. On February 1, 1876, Sitting Bull was officially declared "hostile" by the War Department.

In the spring, General Philip Sheridan launched a three-sided offensive against the hostile Sioux and Cheyenne. General Alfred Terry marched west from North Dakota with 925 men, including Custer and the Seventh Cavalry. Colonel John Gibbon marched east across Montana with 450 men. General George Crook marched north from Wyoming with 1,000 men and 250 Indian scouts. The Americans believed that there were less than 800 warriors who were not on the reservations. By putting over 2,500 soldiers in the field, Sheridan felt confident of victory.

While the three American forces were marching toward him, Sitting Bull was creating a force of his own. The call went out to all of the Sioux, Cheyenne, and Arapaho west of the Missouri River—including those who were living on reservations—to join Sitting Bull in his battle against the white man. By June more than 10,000 Indians were living in a great camp on Rosebud Creek in southeastern Montana. They included between 2,500 and 4,000 warriors. Half of the warriors were armed with outdated rifles; the other half had bows and arrows.

In the middle of June, Sitting Bull participated in the Sun Dance—the most important religious ritual of the Sioux. Before

7

performing the dance, he sacrificed 100 small pieces of flesh from his body. Then bleeding, hungry, and exhausted, he had a vision of soldiers falling from the sky upside down. The meaning of this vision was clear. The soldiers would be killed as they entered the Sioux camp. It would be a great victory.

A few days later, on June 17, 1,000 Sioux warriors drove off 1,250 men under General Crook in the Rosebud valley. Sitting Bull was still exhausted from the Sun Dance, and Crazy Horse led the warriors. This was the largest battle yet fought between the Americans and the Sioux. Crook was amazed by the strength of the Indians, who fought together as they had never fought before. And there were many more warriors than he had expected. He guessed—correctly—that there were even more at their camp.

After the battle, the Indians moved to the Little Big Horn River, which they called the Greasy Grass. Although the Battle of the Rosebud was a great success, Sitting Bull was convinced that there was another battle to come. His vision had been clear: The soldiers would die as they came into his camp. The Battle of the Rosebud had been over 20 miles from the camp.

On June 25, 1876, the Seventh Cavalry under Custer drew near the Indian village. General Terry had ordered Custer to approach the village from the south, while Terry approached it from the north. But Custer—eager for glory—decided to attack the village himself. Around noon Custer divided his forces into three units. He sent Captain Frederick W. Benteen with 125 men toward the south, as General Terry had ordered. Then Major Marcus A. Reno, with 140 men, and Custer, with about 200 men, marched directly toward the Indian village.

Around 2:00 P.M., Custer ordered Reno to chase a group of 40 or 50 Indians down the Little Big Horn River. Reno's men rode into the Hunkpapa camp and surprised the Sioux. But the Indians quickly recovered and drove the soldiers out of the camp, across the river, and onto a hill, killing or wounding about one-third of the soldiers. Finally Benteen's detachment arrived and protected Reno's men until both groups of soldiers could take defensive positions on the hill.

Around the same time, Custer and his men rode directly toward the other end of the village, across from the Cheyenne camp. Before they could cross the river, they were met by a large force of Cheyenne under Crazy Horse and then a large force of Sioux under Gall. Although it is unclear exactly what happened, Custer and all his men were killed. Sitting Bull's vision was fulfilled.

Sitting Bull

According to a number of Indians who were at the Little Big Horn , Sitting Bull fought against Reno and Benteen but did not actually fight against Custer. He watched the battle from a hill on the other side of the river, where the women and children had fled for safety. As chief, his responsibility was to the tribe as a whole. He suspected that Custer's attack might be part of a trap; he could not believe that a man would be stupid enough to attack a force over 10 times larger than his own.

Of course the American public did not consider George Armstrong Custer stupid. They considered him a hero for getting himself and all his men killed. They called the battle Custer's Massacre or Custer's Last Stand, even though he was actually attacking the Indian village. Pressure increased to defeat the Sioux. In September, General Crook's soldiers destroyed a Sioux village at Slim Buttes, despite an attempt by Sitting Bull to bring reinforcements. Crook then marched on and occupied the Black Hills.

While Crook and Sitting Bull were fighting, the Indians living near the agencies were forced to sign an agreement giving up the Black Hills. They had little choice—it was sign or starve. In August, three weeks after Custer's defeat, the U.S. Congress had passed a law that the government agents would not distribute food and supplies until the Sioux gave up the Black Hills. The government was no longer concerned with the promises of the past. The white men wanted the gold of the Black Hills—and they got it.

During the fall of 1876, Sitting Bull and Crazy Horse continued to harass the Americans. When Colonel Nelson Miles established a winter camp on the Yellowstone, Sitting Bull's warriors attacked a supply train and left a note in the middle of the Plains. This is what it said:

> *I want to know what you are doing on this road. You scare all the buffalo away. I want to hunt in this place. I want you to turn back from here. If you don't, I will fight you again. I want you to leave what you have got here and turn back from here.*
> *I am your friend.*
>
> *Sitting Bull*

In October, Colonel Miles and Sitting Bull met on the Plains. Their first discussion was polite, with Miles making a genuine attempt to understand the Indians' point of view. "I never thought that I was against the white man," said Sitting Bull, "but I admit

9

Sitting Bull with his mother, daughter, and granddaughter.
(Arizona Historical Society/Tucson)

I am not for him . . . All I am looking for is to see how and where I can find more meat for my people, more game animals for my people, and to find what God has given me to eat."

The next day both men became angry and their discussion ended quickly. Miles ordered his soldiers to attack the Sioux, and they fought for two days. Finally, about 2,000 of Sitting Bull's followers agreed to go with Miles to an agency. Sitting Bull and the rest of his people moved on to new hunting grounds, and an important opportunity for peace was lost.

In January 1877, Colonel Miles successfully attacked Crazy Horse's camp. This was very discouraging to the Indians. It seemed that they were never safe from the soldiers and big guns of the white man—not even in the middle of winter. On May 6, 1877, Crazy Horse surrendered. A few months later, he was killed while being taken to prison.

Around the time that Crazy Horse surrendered, Sitting Bull led his followers into Canada. The Canadian government promised to protect the Sioux as long as they obeyed the laws, but it would not give them a reservation or economic support. At first life was good in Canada, but in time the Sioux became hungry and homesick. The great buffalo herds were smaller now, and they grazed on the

Sitting Bull

American side of the imaginary line that the white man called a "border." When the warriors crossed the border to hunt the buffalo, American soldiers chased them back to Canada. Which was worse, the blue-coated soldiers or an empty belly?

Slowly Sitting Bull's followers drifted back to the United States. At least at the agencies they would receive a little food—not much, but enough to keep them from starving. Finally the chief decided to take the rest of his people home. On July 19, 1881, Sitting Bull surrendered with 187 followers at Fort Buford in northern Dakota Territory. Before the agent would give them food, they had to give up their horses and guns.

While his followers were sent to the Standing Rock Agency, Sitting Bull was held a prisoner of war at Fort Randall. Two years later he was released and sent to Standing Rock, where he made his camp on the Grand River, not far from the place where he had been born. Although he was happy to be home, Sitting Bull immediately found himself in conflict with the Indian agent, Major James McLaughlin. McLaughlin was one of the better agents, but he was a strong-willed man who was trying to carry out government policy. And government policy was to destroy the Indians' culture by destroying the chiefs' power. McLaughlin refused to acknowledge Sitting Bull's position as head chief. Instead he gave official authority to a number of lesser chiefs who were more willing to follow the white man's ways.

Ironically, the American public *did* recognize Sitting Bull's position. The man who was once considered the hated killer of Custer now became the most famous and popular Indian in the United States. In 1885 he toured with Buffalo Bill's Wild West show and learned more about the white man's world. Disturbed by the poverty in the big cities, he gave most of the money he earned to poor children who gathered around him.

After signing away the Black Hills, the Sioux still had a huge reservation covering most of western South Dakota. In the 1880s, farmers and ranchers wanted that land opened for white settlement. The government offered to buy half the reservation—almost 11 million acres—for 50 cents an acre, later raising the offer to $1.25 an acre. Sitting Bull resisted the sale to the very end. But after pressure from government commissioners and agents—and a promise of more food—the Sioux signed the agreement in 1889. The remaining land was divided into six smaller reservations, including Standing Rock. The Great Sioux Reservation no longer existed.

Once the agreement was signed, the government actually cut the food rations instead of raising them. Faced with starvation and misery, the Sioux looked for another answer to their problems. They found it in the Ghost Dance, a religious movement started in Nevada by a Paiute Indian named Wovoka. Wovoka preached that the dance would lead to eternal youth and happiness for Indians and whites together in a heavenly paradise. But two Sioux medicine men, Short Bull and Kicking Bear, transformed Wovoka's original message into a more warlike, antiwhite movement that helped ease the deep frustration of the Sioux.

The Ghost Dance created hysteria among the whites, who were afraid that the Sioux would leave the reservations and attack white settlements. Although Sitting Bull danced the Ghost Dance, it is doubtful he was a true believer. However, Major McLaughlin saw the Ghost Dance hysteria as a way to get rid of Sitting Bull, whom he considered to be the main obstacle in the way of progress.

McLaughlin reported the situation to General Nelson Miles, military commander of the district that included the Standing Rock Agency. Sixteen years earlier Miles had met with Sitting Bull to discuss peace on the northern Plains. Now he ordered McLaughlin to arrest the old chief. Although army troops were available to assist him, McLaughlin insisted on handling the situation with his Indian police—a hand-picked force of Sioux who helped the agent control the other Sioux on the reservation.

At dawn on December 15, 1890, 43 Indian policemen arrived at Sitting Bull's camp and arrested the chief. A bloody fight broke out between Sitting Bull's followers and the policemen. When it was over, Sitting Bull was dead along with seven of his followers. Four Indian policemen were killed, and two more died of their wounds.

The death of Sitting Bull increased the tension between Indians and whites in South Dakota. Exactly two weeks later, on December 29, 1890, U.S. soldiers killed at least 146 Sioux at Wounded Knee. The dead included 44 women and 18 children. Twenty-five soldiers were also killed. It was the last armed uprising of the American Indians in the 19th century.

Sitting Bull was one of the greatest—if not the greatest—of all American Indian leaders. He combined the courage of a great warrior with the thoughtful intelligence of a great statesman. He loved his people like a father and believed that Wakan Tanka—the Great Spirit—had entrusted them to his care. He had no need for the white man or the white man's ways. He asked only to be left alone.

But of course he could not be left alone. His land lay directly in the path of progress. Gold, farms, ranches, railroads—all these brought the white man to the land of the Sioux. Sitting Bull and his people were fortunate that they lived in the wilderness of the northern Plains; they were able to live their traditional life longer than most Indians. But once the white man came, even a great leader like Sitting Bull could not stop him.

Sitting Bull was deeply loved and respected by his people. An American named Frank Grouard was captured by the Sioux and lived with the tribe for several years. Grouard later said: "The name of Sitting Bull was a 'tipi word' for all that was generous and great. The bucks admired him, the squaws respected him highly, and the children loved him . . . No man in the Sioux nation was braver than Sitting Bull."

Major James McLaughlin, the Indian agent who fought with the chief for control of his people and ultimately caused his death, admitted that Sitting Bull was "by far the most influential man of his nation for many years." It was this influence that was so threatening to the white man. As long as Sitting Bull was alive, the old life of the Sioux lived with him.

Chronology

c. March 1831	Sitting Bull is born near the Grand River in present-day South Dakota
1856	Kills a Crow chief in one-on-one combat
July 28, 1864	Fights U.S. troops at Kildeer Mountain
November 29, 1864	U.S. troops massacre Cheyenne women and children at Sand Creek, Colorado
September 1865	Sitting Bull and 400 warriors drive U.S. troops from Powder River country
c. 1867/68	Sitting Bull is chosen head chief of Teton Sioux who want to continue fighting
July–Nov. 1868	Some Sioux leaders sign Treaty of 1868 establishing Great Sioux Reservation
Summer 1874	Custer leads expedition to Black Hills; starts gold rush
Spring 1876	U.S. troops search for the Sioux; Sitting Bull is building large force on Rosebud Creek
June 17, 1876	Battle of Rosebud; 1,000 Sioux warriors drive off 1,250 U.S. soldiers
June 25, 1876	Battle of the Little Big Horn; Sioux and allies kill Custer and 200 men
September 1876	Sioux at agencies are forced to sign away the Black Hills
May 1877	Crazy Horse surrenders; Sitting Bull leads his followers to Canada
July 19, 1881	Sitting Bull surrenders at Fort Buford, Dakota Territory
July 1889	Sioux are forced to sell half of their reservation
December 15, 1890	Sitting Bull is killed by Indian policemen

Further Reading

Young Adult Books

Black, Sheila. *Sitting Bull and the Battle of the Little Big Horn*. Englewood Cliffs, NJ: Silver Burdett Press, 1989. The most recent young adult biography; includes illustrations and bibliography; 130 pp.

Garst, Doris Shannon. *Sitting Bull, Champion of His People*. New York: Julian Messner Inc., 1946. A popular full-length young adult biography; includes illustrations; 189 pp.

O'Connor, Richard. *Sitting Bull, War Chief of the Sioux*. New York: McGraw-Hill, 1968. A full-length young adult biography; includes illustrations; 144 pp.

Adult Books

Adams, Alexander B. *Sitting Bull, An Epic of the Plains*. New York: G. P. Putnam's Sons, 1973. Despite its title, this is more of a history than a biography; it provides an excellent overview of the conflict between the Sioux and the U.S. government; the style is clear but it may be too detailed for young readers.

Vestal, Stanley. *Sitting Bull: Champion of the Sioux*, revised edition. Norman: University of Oklahoma Press, 1957. Original edition published by Houghton Mifflin Company, 1932. A detailed biography based on interviews with Indians who fought with Sitting Bull; it provides an excellent portrait of Sitting Bull's character as well as the Indians' point of view in their conflict with the United States; the style is clear enough for some young readers.

Jesse James:
The Life and the Legend

Jesse James. This photo was probably taken around the time of Jesse's marriage to Zerelda "Zee" Mimms in April 1874.
(Western History Collections, University of Oklahoma Library; Rose Collection)

---

*T*he pretty, tired woman began to cry as she spoke to the two strangers. "I'm glad you enjoyed your dinner," she said, "because it's the last meal we'll ever eat on this farm. The sheriff is coming this afternoon to foreclose our mortgage and throw us off the land. He's a Northern carpetbagger and he has no sympathy for the widow of a Confederate soldier and her five children."

"Don't cry, gentle woman," said one of the strangers.

"How much is the mortgage?" asked the other.

"Eight hundred dollars," replied the widow. "Where on earth could I ever find that kind of money?"

The woman didn't know it, but her two mysterious dinner guests were Frank and Jesse James. They had just robbed the bank at Gallatin, and their saddlebags were stuffed with cash. "I just happen to have eight hundred dollars," said Jesse. "I'll loan you the money for the mortgage. Don't worry about paying me back."

A few hours later, the James brothers were back on the road when they noticed a sour-looking fellow riding away from the widow's farm. Frank asked the man who he was.

"I'm the county sheriff," was the reply. "What's your business?"

As quick as lightning, Jesse and Frank had the sheriff covered with their Navy Colts. "Hand over all your money," Jesse ordered.

The sheriff handed the outlaws a wad of bills from his saddlebag. Jesse and Frank laughed at the sight of the money. It was their eight hundred dollars.

This is one of the most famous stories in the legend of Jesse James. It is told in many different versions, but the basic idea is the same: Jesse James is portrayed as an American Robin Hood, stealing from the rich bank (or railroad) and helping the poor Confederate widow. And, like Robin Hood, he is so clever that he steals the money back from the evil sheriff.

The image of Jesse James as a dashing Robin Hood began during his lifetime and has continued for more than a century since his death. Although it makes for a good story, it does not reflect the real life of Jesse James. Jesse and his brother, Frank, were intelligent men who exhibited a dashing, romantic style in their crimes. But there is no evidence that their robberies benefited anyone but themselves. And the legend conveniently ignores the long trail of dead bodies the James gang left behind.

Jesse Woodson James was born September 5, 1847, on a farm in Clay County, Missouri. His older brother, Alexander Franklin (Frank) James, was born January 10, 1843. The James boys were the sons of a Baptist minister. When Jesse was three years old, the Reverend James left his family for the goldfields of California, only to die a few weeks after he arrived. Mrs. James remarried, divorced, and remarried again. Her third husband was Dr. Reuben

Samuel, a farmer/physician who was apparently a good stepfather to Jesse and Frank.

During the Civil War (1861–65), the people of Missouri were split between those who supported the Union and those who supported the Confederacy. Missouri's regular Confederate troops were defeated quickly, but irregular troops called guerrillas continued to fight bloody battles with the Union forces throughout the war. Men on both sides often acted more like criminals than soldiers.

By 1863 Frank James had joined a band of Confederate guerrillas under William C. Quantrill—the famed Quantrill's Raiders. On August 21, 1863, Frank took part in Quantrill's raid on Lawrence, Kansas, in which 150 unarmed men and boys were killed and much of the town was burned to the ground. The following year Frank joined a group commanded by Quantrill's lieutenant, William "Bloody Bill" Anderson. Jesse James, not quite 17, also rode with Anderson.

On September 27, 1864, Anderson's men stopped a train in Centralia, Missouri, by piling railroad ties on the track. They stole $3,000 from the express car; then they lined up and shot 24 unarmed Union soldiers who were among the passengers. Later, the guerrillas were pursued by Union troops. In a lopsided battle, Anderson's raiders killed over 100 Union soldiers while losing only three men. Young Jesse James was credited with killing the Union commander.

At the end of the war, most Confederate guerrillas—including Frank James—surrendered officially to the Union army. According to legend, Jesse was shot and wounded by Union soldiers while attempting to surrender under a white flag of truce. This story may or may not be true, but Jesse was severely wounded around this time with a bullet in his chest. During his long period of recovery, he was nursed by a cousin named Zerelda "Zee" Mimms. Jesse and Zee fell in love and promised to marry.

The wound in Jesse's chest took almost a year to heal; the wounds of the Civil War took much longer. For five years after the war, Missouri was governed by Radical Republicans who viewed Confederate sympathizers as criminals. Former Confederate guerrillas were not allowed to vote or to work in professions such as law or medicine. Despite these restrictions, many Confederate guerrillas settled down and lived peaceful lives. Others became outlaws.

Jesse James

On February 13, 1866, two men entered the Clay County Savings Bank in Liberty, Missouri. One of them stepped up to the cashier, asked for change for a $10 bill, pulled out a six-shooter, and added, "I'd like all the money in the bank." The men left the bank carrying a large wheat sack stuffed with almost $60,000 in currency, bonds, gold, and silver. The bandits mounted their horses and joined their accomplices, forming a group of 10 to 12 heavily armed men. On their way out of town, the outlaws shot and killed a college student who happened to be standing on the street.

This was the first daylight bank robbery in America during peacetime. Over the next two years, a gang of five or six men committed three similar bank robberies in Missouri and one in Kentucky. At Richmond, Missouri, three citizens were killed while trying to resist the outlaws.

The James brothers were not accused of these crimes, and they were not mentioned in the original newspaper accounts or legal documents of the time. However, western historians believe that Frank and Jesse James participated in some or all of the robberies from 1866 to 1868. In 1869 the situation became clearer.

On December 7, 1869, two men entered the Daviess County Savings Bank in Gallatin, Missouri. One of them asked the cashier to change a $100 bill. The other asked him to write out a receipt. As the cashier began to write, the first man shot and killed him. By this time the townspeople had been alerted to the robbery. Grabbing a few hundred dollars, the outlaws ran out of the bank and faced a barrage of gunfire. The men tried to mount their horses, but one of the animals grew skittish from the gunfire. Finally both outlaws escaped on a single horse. The horse that had been left behind was identified as belonging to Jesse James.

A sheriff's posse went to the James farm, only to be surprised by Jesse and Frank riding at full speed out of the stables, over a high fence, and disappearing into the woods. The James brothers had begun their life on the run.

Six months after the robbery, a letter—supposedly written by Jesse James—appeared in the Kansas City *Times*. The writer claimed that Jesse was not guilty of the murder and robbery in Gallatin, but that he would not surrender until he was sure he would receive a fair trial. He pointed out that other former Confederate guerrillas—who had been captured and accused of the earlier bank robberies—had been hanged by mobs before receiving a trial. This was the first of many similar letters that appeared like clockwork after other James crimes.

The editor of the Kansas City *Times* was a former Confederate soldier named John Newman Edwards. Like many Confederate sympathizers, Edwards believed that Frank and Jesse James were good men who were being persecuted for their actions during the Civil War. During the 13 years that the James brothers were on the run, he wrote many editorials and articles defending them. It is interesting that as Edwards moved from one newspaper to another, the letters from Jesse moved with him.

On June 3, 1871, four men robbed a bank in Corydon, Iowa, of $6,000. On the way out of town, the gang stopped at a Methodist church where most of the townspeople were listening to a speech about the coming of the railroad. The leader of the gang interrupted the speech and said, "We've just been down to the bank and taken every dollar in the till." By the time the townspeople realized that he wasn't kidding, the gang was gone.

Based on their descriptions, the four robbers were believed to be Jesse James, Frank James, Cole Younger, and Clell Miller. Cole Younger was the oldest of four brothers; the others were John, Jim, and Bob. Like the James brothers, the Younger brothers were from a good family who supported the Confederacy during the Civil War. At various times all four Youngers rode with the James gang.

One of the gang's most daring robberies took place in September 1872. Three men—believed to be the James brothers and Bob Younger—rode up to the ticket booth of the Kansas City Fair. In the midst of 10,000 people, they demanded the tin cash box. When the ticket seller resisted, one of the robbers fired at him and missed, hitting a young girl in the leg. The robbers rode away through the crowd, escaping with a grand total of $978.

John Edwards wrote an editorial entitled "The Chivalry of Crime" in which he compared the robbers to the Knights of the Round Table in the legend of King Arthur. "What they did we condemn," wrote Edwards. "But the way they did it we cannot help admiring . . . It was as though three bandits had come to us . . . with the halo of medieval chivalry upon their garments and shown us how the things were done that poets sing of." Edwards conveniently ignored the little girl with the bullet in her leg.

In July 1873, the James gang turned to a new form of crime. A group of five to seven men loosened a train track near Council Bluffs, Iowa. When the train arrived, the engine ran off the track and fell on its side, crushing the engineer. The robbers broke into the express safe, which contained only $2,000. Angry with the small take, they robbed the passengers before escaping into the night. Apparently the gang robbed the wrong train. The next morning another train passed carrying a large shipment of gold bullion.

Six months later the James gang tried again. At Gads Hill, Missouri, five men took over the train station, stopped the train with a signal flag, and stole an estimated $2,000 to $22,000 from the express safe. In the passenger car, the robbers examined the hands of each male passenger. "Hard-handed men have to work for their money," the leader explained. "The soft-handed ones are capitalists, professors, and others that get money easy." The bandits stole from the soft-handed, easy-money passengers and passed by the hard-handed workers. Although this was the only robbery in which the James gang distinguished between rich and poor, it helped to establish the American Robin Hood legend.

At a time when there was no FBI and little communication between local sheriffs, the Pinkerton Detective Agency was the most effective law enforcement agency in the country. The Pinkertons had been on the trail of the gang since 1871. After the Gads Hill train robbery, the detectives became convinced that the mysterious robbers were the James and Younger brothers. On March 10, 1874, a Pinkerton detective arrived in Clay County and headed for the James farm, intending to infiltrate the family by working as a farmhand. He was found dead the next morning, lying along a road many miles away from the farm.

A few days later, two other Pinkerton detectives arrived and convinced a former deputy sheriff to help them find the outlaws. The three men got into a shooting battle with John and Jim Younger. When it was over, John Younger and the former sheriff were dead, and one of the Pinkertons was fatally wounded.

The next month, on April 24, 1874, Jesse James married his cousin Zee Mimms, after a nine-year engagement. Despite his career as an outlaw, Jesse and Zee had a loving marriage. Around the time of Jesse's marriage, Frank James secretly married Annie Ralston.

With the election of 1874 approaching, the James/Younger gang became a hot political issue. By this time the state was governed by the Democratic party. Many Democrats were former Confederates who were naturally sympathetic toward the ex-guerrillas. The Republican newspapers in Missouri, as well as papers in other states, accused the Democrats of protecting the James/Younger

*Jesse's wife, Zee, posing with Jesse's guns shortly after
the death of her infamous husband. Apparently Zee
knew very little about Jesse's illegal activities during
his life.*
(Western History Collections, University of Oklahoma
Library; Rose Collection)

gang. They called Missouri "the Bandit State" and "Poor Old
Missouri."

On January 26, 1875, Pinkerton detectives threw a firebomb
into the living room of Jesse's mother and stepfather, Dr. Samuel.
When Dr. Samuel kicked the bomb into the fireplace, it exploded,
killing Jesse's nine-year-old half-brother, Archie Samuel, and
mangling Jesse's mother's right hand so badly that it had to be

amputated. This tragedy turned public opinion against the Pinkertons and increased sympathy for the James brothers. A few
months later a neighbor suspected of helping the Pinkertons was
gunned down on his doorstep.

Although they were suspected of crimes from West Virginia to
Texas, the James/Younger gang had never been positively identified. Few people really knew what the James and Younger brothers looked like, and those who did know refused to cooperate with
authorities. That changed in the summer of 1876. A group of men
robbed a train at Rocky Cut, Missouri, and escaped with $15,000.
A newcomer to the gang named Hobbs Kerry was arrested and
confessed to the crime, naming his accomplices: Jesse James,
Frank James, Cole Younger, Bob Younger, Clell Miller, Charlie
Pitts, and Bill Chadwell.

Feeling pressure on their home ground, the gang set their sights
to the north. Eight men—Jim Younger and the seven named by
Hobbs Kerry—headed for Minnesota. On September 7, 1876, they
rode into the town of Northfield. Three men waited on the outskirts of town, two guarded the street outside the bank, and three
entered the First National Bank. When the cashier resisted, one
of the bandits cut his throat and shot him. A bank teller was shot
in the shoulder but escaped out a window and alerted the town.

The citizens of Northfield resisted as no one had resisted before,
firing at the outlaws from positions throughout the town. The two
outlaws guarding the bank killed a young Swedish man who didn't
understand their command to get out of the way. Hearing the
shooting, the three outlaws on the outskirts of town rode in to help
their comrades. The fighting in the town square grew hotter, with
bullets raining from both sides. Six bandits escaped, but Bill
Chadwell and Clell Miller lay dead in the street. Most of the others
were wounded.

In the past the James/Younger gang had easily disappeared into
the Missouri countryside. But now they were in a strange state
hundreds of miles from home, where the people were not sympathetic to former Confederate guerrillas. A huge manhunt was
organized, and the outlaws were pursued like hunted animals. The
gang split, with Jesse and Frank riding off alone. A few days later,
a posse found the Youngers and Charlie Pitts. In a bloody battle,
Pitts was killed and the three Younger brothers—wounded, cold,
and beaten—were captured. Expecting to be strung up by a mob,
the Youngers pleaded guilty and gratefully accepted life impris-
onment in the Minnesota penitentiary.

After the Northfield disaster, the James brothers apparently retired temporarily from crime. From around 1875—before the Northfield raid—until 1881, they lived in Nashville, Tennessee, under assumed names. Jesse was J. D. Howard; Frank was B. J. Woodson. Jesse worked at a variety of jobs, including farming, hauling, and trading in grain. Jesse and Zee's two children were born during this period: Jesse Edwards in December 1875 and Mary in July 1879. Frank and Annie's only child, Robert Franklin, was born in 1878.

There are many reports of the James brothers appearing throughout the West during this period. Most of them are rumors and legends, but two interesting stories are quite possible. In July 1879, Jesse may have visited Billy the Kid in Las Vegas, New Mexico. This is established by a reliable witness who had dinner with the two famous outlaws. In April 1881—when he was back on the run—Jesse apparently hid at Belle Starr's ranch in the Indian Territory. Jesse knew Belle through Cole Younger.

On October 8, 1879, a group of men forced the station agent at Glendale, Missouri, to change a signal and stop a train. While some of the bandits boarded the train and robbed the express car, the others shot along the sides of the passenger cars, thus preventing the curious passengers from watching the robbery. The style of the robbery convinced the people of Missouri that the James gang was back in business.

Frank James was not involved in the Glendale robbery, but in March 1881 he and Jesse apparently led the robbery of a U.S. government paymaster. In July the James gang robbed a train near Winston, Missouri. The bandits boarded the train at two separate stops and quietly spread out among the passengers. A tall man with a heavy black beard—apparently Jesse James—surprised the conductor and shot him twice from behind; as he died he fell out of the train. Then the bearded outlaw and another man—apparently Frank James—shot and killed a passenger. Two outlaws went to the express car, where they savagely beat the guard and stole an unknown amount of money and valuables from the safe. The rest of the gang forced the engineer to stop, and the gang jumped off the train.

The double murder aroused the anger of the people of Missouri. Times had changed, and the crimes of the James brothers could no longer be blamed on the Civil War. Although John Edwards continued to defend them, most newspapers and public officials demanded their capture. Governor Thomas Crittenden organized the railroad and express company officials and offered rewards of $5,000 for their conviction in the Winston or Glendale train robberies, and $5,000 for the arrest and conviction of other participants in the crimes. These were extremely large rewards for that time. Governor Crittenden believed that the other gang members would be tempted to betray the James brothers.

The James gang robbed one more train before the plan began to work. On September 7, 1881, they stopped a train at Blue Cut, Missouri, by blocking the tracks with logs. After robbing the express car and over 100 passengers, Jesse gave the engineer two silver dollars and said, "You are a brave man . . . Here is two dollars for you to drink [to] the health of Jesse James tomorrow morning."

A few weeks after the Blue Cut robbery, an outlaw named William Ryan was sentenced to 25 years in prison for robbing the Glendale train. The main witness against Ryan was another gang member named Tucker Bassham who had been pardoned by Governor Crittenden in return for his testimony. In January 1882, gang member Dick Liddil surrendered. Liddil had been involved in all the gang activities since the Glendale robbery and was willing to testify in return for the governor's protection. In February, a cousin of the James brothers named Clarence Hite was arrested. Knowing that Liddil would testify against him, Hite pleaded guilty to the Winston robbery and was sentenced to 25 years in prison. The gang was falling apart.

By this time Jesse James was living with his wife and children in St. Joseph, Missouri under the name Thomas Howard. Living with the "Howard" family were two "cousins," Charles and Bob Ford. Jesse was planning a robbery with the Ford brothers. He didn't know that they had promised Governor Crittenden to deliver Jesse James for the reward.

On the morning of April 3, 1882, Jesse and the Ford brothers ate breakfast and read the newspapers. One of the papers contained news of Dick Liddil's surrender, and Jesse became suspicious that the Ford brothers would betray him just as Liddil had done. Although the reward was for Jesse alive, the Fords panicked and looked for a chance to kill him. After breakfast—for reasons that have never been explained—Jesse took off his guns and stepped up onto a chair to dust and straighten a picture. Bob Ford drew his revolver and shot the unarmed outlaw in the back of the head. Jesse James fell to the floor and died.

The news of Jesse's death flashed across the country. Although Governor Crittenden was praised for ending the outlaw's career, he was criticized for using an assassin. Many stolen objects were found among Jesse's possessions, tying him to robberies that he had only been suspected of before. Despite this evidence, the fact that Jesse was shot in the back made people sympathetic toward the outlaw and helped to continue the Robin Hood legend.

Jesse James shortly after being shot from behind by Robert Ford. At the time of his death, Jesse's name was known throughout the country, but few people had actually seen his face.
(National Archives. Photograph by R. Uhlman, St. Joseph, Missouri)

Six months later, on October 5, 1882, Frank James surrendered to Governor Crittenden. Although he was tried twice—once in Missouri, once in Alabama—he was never convicted. His reputation as a Confederate hero proved strong enough to overcome the facts of his crimes. By 1885 he was released from custody and lived the rest of his life as an honest citizen. Frank James died on February 18, 1915, in the room where he was born.

The Younger brothers' Confederate past did not help them in Minnesota. Bob Younger died of tuberculosis in prison in 1889. Cole and Jim Younger were finally paroled in 1901, after 25 years behind bars. Jim committed suicide the following year. Cole Younger returned to Missouri in 1903 and became a popular public speaker, giving lectures entitled "Crime Does Not Pay" and "What Life Has Taught Me." He died in 1916.

Jesse James was not an American Robin Hood, and the James/Younger gang were not the Merry Men. But they continue to be the most famous outlaws in the history of American crime. Part of their appeal is simply the fact that they were the first great outlaw gang of the Wild West. Their methods were copied by other western gangs into the 20th century—gangs such as Butch Cassidy and the Wild Bunch.

However, the most important reason for the continuing appeal of Jesse James is his image as a brave Confederate soldier who kept on fighting because he wasn't allowed to live in peace. In his biography, *Jesse James Was His Name*, William A. Settle writes, "While there is no one simple explanation of the making of the James legend, the James band's career of lawlessness and the growth of the legend around it are deeply rooted in . . . the events of the Civil War and its aftermath." Settle points out that Missouri—more than any other state—was torn by intense feelings on both sides of the conflict, feelings that elevated a group of cold criminals to the status of heroes.

Less than two weeks after Jesse James was gunned down by Bob Ford, a newspaper story announced that some people believed Jesse was not really dead, that the killing was a hoax to allow him to escape. During the next 66 years, at least 30 different people claimed to be the "real" Jesse James. The last one was a 101-year-old man named J. Frank Dalton who staked his claim in 1948. The phony Jesses emphasize the truth of the Jesse James story. The man died in 1882; the legend lives on.

Chronology

September 5, 1847	Jesse Woodson James is born in Clay County, Missouri
September 27, 1864	Anderson's guerrillas—including the James brothers—rob train and murder Union soldiers at Centralia, Missouri
February 13, 1866	Robbery of the Clay County Savings Bank in Liberty, Missouri
December 7, 1869	James brothers rob bank in Gallatin, Missouri, and kill cashier
September 26, 1872	Robbery of the ticket booth at the Kansas City Fair
July 21, 1873	James/Younger gang rob a train near Council Bluffs, Iowa
April 24, 1874	Jesse James marries Zerelda (Zee) Mimms
January 26, 1875	Pinkerton firebomb explodes in the Samuels' living room
September 7, 1876	Attempted robbery in Northfield, Minnesota; Younger brothers are later captured
October 8, 1879	Train robbery at Glendale, Missouri
April 3, 1882	Jesse James is shot and killed by Bob Ford in St. Joseph, Missouri
October 5, 1882	Frank James surrenders

Further Reading

Young Adult Books
Baldwin, Margaret, and Pat O'Brien. *Wanted! Frank and Jesse James: The Real Story*. New York: Julian Messner, 1981. An excellent full-length young adult biography that attempts to separate fact from fiction; includes bibliography, index, and photographs; 191 pp.

Adult Books
Settle, William A. *Jesse James Was His Name*. Columbia: University of Missouri Press, 1966. The best full-length biography; too difficult for young readers but excellent for checking facts; includes extensive notes and bibliography.

Trachtman, Paul. *The Gunfighters*, pp. 52–89. Series: The Old West. Alexandria, VA: Time-Life Books, 1974. A good account written in language that young readers will understand; many illustrations.

Buffalo Bill:
Scout and Showman

William F. "Buffalo Bill" Cody.
(Western History Collections, University of
Oklahoma Library; Rose Collection)

*B*uffalo Bill rides into the arena on his big white stallion. He sits tall and straight in the saddle, a ten-gallon hat on his head, his long brown hair flowing in the wind. In his right hand he carries a huge American flag. The crowd cheers as he rides toward

Victoria, the queen of England. As Bill brings his horse to a halt, the queen stands and bows politely to the flag. It is the first time in history that an English sovereign has publicly recognized the American flag.

This was one of the finest moments in the long career of William F. Cody, the man known around the world as Buffalo Bill. It is symbolic of Cody's importance to the history of the Wild West, for it was through Buffalo Bill's Wild West show that the American West became famous in England and Europe. But Buffalo Bill was more than a great entertainer. He was a rugged frontiersman who lived the life he portrayed in his show.

William Frederick Cody was born on February 26, 1846, in Scott County, Iowa. His father, Isaac Cody, was a farmer and Indian trader. When Bill was seven, his older brother, Samuel, died after a fall from a horse, leaving Bill as the oldest son. The following spring, in April 1854, the family moved to Kansas, which was just being opened for white settlement.

As settlers poured into the new territory, there was violent conflict between those who wanted Kansas to be a slave state and those who wanted it to be a free state. Isaac Cody became active in the Free State movement and was stabbed while making a speech. Although he recovered, the wound contributed to his death in 1857.

At the age of 11, Bill was the man of the family, which included his mother, five sisters, and one brother. He went to work as an errand boy for Majors & Russell, a freight company transporting supplies for the U.S. Army. After a few months, he joined a company wagon train across the Plains and made several trips over the next few years. By the time he was 13, Bill had learned to hunt buffalo and killed an Indian. He spent one winter at Fort Bridger, where he met the great scouts Jim Bridger and Kit Carson. During this period Bill also met James B. Hickok, who later became famous as "Wild Bill."

In 1859 Cody attended school for two and a half months, the longest period of schooling he ever had. He learned to read and write, although his spelling was always poor. In 1860 Bill joined the Pony Express, an experimental mail service that was operated by his old employers, now called Russell, Majors, and Waddell. Using a series of riders—who each used a series of horses—the

Express carried mail from St. Joseph, Missouri, to Sacramento, California. At 14, Bill Cody may have been the youngest Pony Express rider. He made the third longest ride in the history of the Express: 322 miles in less than 22 hours, using 21 different horses.

When the Civil War began in 1861, Cody returned to Leavenworth, Kansas and joined a group of Union supporters who stole horses from Missouri. In February 1864, he enlisted in the Seventh Kansas Volunteer Cavalry and served for over a year and a half, fighting in a number of important battles in Missouri and Mississippi. After the war, Cody guided General William Sherman through Kansas and Nebraska. He then worked for a time as a stagecoach driver on the famous Overland Stage Line.

On March 6, 1866, Cody married Louisa Frederici in St. Louis. She was a proper young lady of a good family and a sophisticated city. To the rough young man of the Plains, she was the most beautiful woman he had ever seen. Unfortunately, Louisa didn't like the West, and she didn't like show business. The Codys had four children and were married for over 50 years, but they spent very little time together.

After their marriage, Cody and Louisa returned to the Leavenworth area, where he attempted to run his mother's old house as a hotel. His customers loved him, but he was too generous to make money. After six months he sold the hotel and headed for the open spaces of the West, leaving Louisa behind.

At Junction City, Kansas, Cody met his old friend Bill Hickok, who was working as a scout for the army. Cody was also hired as a scout, working out of Fort Ellsworth and Fort Hays. On August 2, 1867, he was involved in his first major Indian fight, with 34 soldiers facing 300 Indians. Shortly after the battle, Cody resigned from scouting and attempted to start a new town, called Rome, along the route of the Kansas Pacific Railroad. Rome died out when the railroad passed it by for a better site.

In the fall of 1867, Cody was hired to provide buffalo meat for the railroad workers. He agreed to deliver 12 buffalo a day for $500 per month—a great deal of money in those days. Cody later wrote that he killed 4,280 buffalo in 18 months. This is probably a printing mistake because of Cody's poor handwriting. It is more likely that he killed 4,280 buffalo in *eight* months, or almost 18 buffalo per day. It was during this period that he became known as "Buffalo Bill."

Because of his famous name, Cody is often connected with the destruction of the buffalo. This is absurd. During his entire life,

Buffalo Bill

Cody killed at most 10,000 buffalo, and he killed them only for food. It was not until the 1870s that the slaughter of the buffalo began. In 1872, hide hunters killed 1.2 *million* buffalo—not for food, but for their skins. This continued until, by 1875, the southern herd—which had once roamed the Plains of Kansas, Nebraska, and Colorado—ceased to exist. By 1883, the northern herd—in Wyoming, Montana, and the Dakotas—was gone as well.

Cody left the buffalo hunting job in May 1868. On September 15, he was hired by General Philip Sheridan as chief of scouts for the Fifth Cavalry. During the next year, Cody participated in seven campaigns against the Plains Indians, including nine battles.

On July 11, 1869, at Summit Springs, Colorado, he guided the troops in a victory over the Cheyenne leader Tall Bull and his warriors, the Dog Soldiers. Cody apparently fired the shot that killed Tall Bull. This battle opened western Kansas and southwestern Nebraska for white settlement.

Shortly afterward Cody met a writer named Edward Judson, who wrote under the pen name Ned Buntline. Buntline wrote dime novels—cheaply printed adventure stories that were published weekly and sold for 5 or 10 cents. After spending a few days with Cody, Buntline wrote a dime novel entitled *Buffalo Bill, the King of the Border Men*. The story was the beginning of Cody's national fame. Strangely enough, the novel is actually based on Wild Bill Hickok's adventures in the Civil War. It had no connection with Cody except the title.

During this period Cody began to lead hunting parties of rich and famous men. It was good public relations for the army—which was spending millions of dollars to make the Plains safe for whites—and Bill Cody was the right man for the job. He was a great storyteller, and he looked the part of the noble frontiersman, with his buckskin suit, long flowing hair, and great white stallion. In January 1872, Cody guided the Grand Duke Alexis, son of Czar Alexander I of Russia. To entertain his royal guest, Cody arranged a "genuine" war dance by a group of friendly Sioux. One newspaper headline proclaimed: "Buffalo Bill as Guide, Tutor, and Entertaining Agent."

After the hunt with Alexis, Cody took a leave of absence from the army and visited the East. By this time a play had been written based on Buntline's novel, and Cody was offered $500 to play himself. He turned it down and returned to Nebraska, where he was once again employed as a scout. Ned Buntline wrote two more Buffalo Bill novels to take advantage of the publicity from Cody's visit.

On April 26, 1872, Cody killed three Indians in a skirmish near the Loup River in Nebraska. His commanding officer reported, "Mr. William Cody's reputation for bravery and skill as a guide is so well established that I need not say anything else but that he acted in his usual manner." Cody was awarded the Medal of Honor, the only medal the U.S. military awarded at that time.

Between his scouting duties, Cody received letters from Ned Buntline urging him to come East and make his fortune as an actor. Cody and Louisa now had three children, and he decided that it was worth a try. In Chicago, on December 18, 1872, William F. Cody made his stage debut in *The Scouts of the Prairie*, a melodrama written by Buntline and based on one of his Buffalo Bill novels. Cody was joined in the cast by another scout named Texas Jack, an Italian actress named Morlacchi, and the versatile Buntline, who was author, actor, manager, and publicity man.

A publicity photo for Scouts of the Prairie, *taken during the 1872–73 season; (l. to r.) Buffalo Bill Cody, Ned Buntline, Texas Jack.*
(Buffalo Bill Memorial Museum, Lookout Mountain, Colorado, City & County of Denver, Denver Mountain Parks)

Buffalo Bill

On his first night, Cody was so nervous that he could not remember a single word of the script. Buntline asked him questions about his real life, and Cody just talked as he always talked. The audience loved him. He was tall and handsome, and he told a good story. The group toured for five months, and newspapers began calling it the "Buffalo Bill troupe." The New York *Herald* said, "Everything is so wonderfully bad, it is almost good." At the end of the season, Cody and Texas Jack decided to split from Buntline.

During the second season, the troupe toured with a new melodrama entitled *The Scouts of the Plains*. It was the same nonsense as the first play, with Buffalo Bill and Texas Jack shooting extras dressed up like Indians and rescuing an Indian maiden with an Italian accent. Buntline was replaced by Cody's old friend Wild Bill Hickok. He was now famous as a Kansas lawman, but he was not meant for the stage. His voice was weak, the lights hurt his eyes, and he liked to shoot his gun too close to the "Indians." After a few months Cody asked Wild Bill to leave the company, and they parted on good terms.

In August 1875, a dime novel appeared entitled *The Pearl of the Prairies; or, the Scout and the Renegade*. This was the first of 22 novels that were supposedly written by Buffalo Bill himself. Many people assumed that Cody used ghostwriters to write under his name; however, there is evidence that he actually wrote at least some of these books, particularly the early ones. In 1879 *The Life of Hon. William F. Cody* was published. This was the first of eight Cody autobiographies and the only one that was written by Cody himself.

On April 20, 1876, Cody's only son, Kit Carson Cody, died of scarlet fever at the age of five. It was the greatest tragedy of Cody's life. Broken-hearted, Cody finished the theater season and rejoined the Fifth Cavalry, which was now part of a large force assembled to drive the Sioux and their allies onto the reservations. On July 17, Cody led a detachment of troopers against a group of Cheyenne warriors. In a one-on-one battle, Cody shot and killed a leader named Yellow Hair. He then scalped the dead Indian, raised the scalp in the air, and shouted, "The first scalp for Custer!" A few weeks earlier, George Armstrong Custer and 200 soldiers had been slaughtered at the Little Big Horn.

The killing of Yellow Hair, who was mistakenly called Yellow *Hand*, became the most famous and controversial event of Cody's military career. The controversy grew because writers and publicity men exaggerated the killing until it was a duel on horseback, with Yellow Hand challenging Cody by name, and the Indians and troopers clearing the field for the battle between the two great warriors. In this form it was reenacted for many years in the Wild West show.

After the military campaign, Cody returned to the stage in a play about the war against the Sioux, including the killing of Yellow Hand. The following summer the Buffalo Bill troupe successfully toured California and the Far West, the first time that a western play was actually performed in the West. After the tour, Cody went to the Sioux reservation and hired a number of "friendly" Indians for the following season. This was the first time he used real Indians in his show, and it was a major step toward the authentic Wild West show.

For the next few years, Cody continued to tour with a new play each season. They were successful financially, but it seemed the audience was more interested in Cody's shooting exhibitions and the genuine Indian dances than in the play. Cody began to form a new idea. In 1882 he met another actor named Nate Salsbury who wanted to take an exhibition of horsemanship to Europe. Cody was interested, but they decided to postpone it for a year or so. That summer he returned to his home in North Platte, Nebraska. On the Fourth of July, Cody staged a celebration called the Old Glory Blow-Out, which was similar to what we would call a rodeo. The event was so successful that he became convinced there was an audience for an outdoor western show.

Nate Salsbury didn't have enough money, so Cody went into partnership with Dr. W. F. Carver, a famous shooting champion. On May 17, 1883, the show gave its first performance at the Omaha Fair Grounds as "The Wild West, Hon. W. F. Cody and Dr. W. F. Carver's Rocky Mountain and Prairie Exhibition." Among the events were an attack on the Deadwood Stage by Indians in war paint, a Pony Express demonstration, horse races, shooting, bucking broncos, and a buffalo hunt. The first season was unsuccessful financially, and Cody and Carver fought bitterly. However, the *Hartford Courant* called it "the best open-air show ever seen."

In the fall of 1883, Cody split with Carver and formed a new partnership with Nate Salsbury. Although he was originally a performer, Salsbury worked behind the scenes to make the show run smoothly. Cody was the director and star performer. During the summer of 1884, they toured under a new name: "Buffalo Bill's

Buffalo Bill

Wild West—America's National Entertainment." The season began well, but that winter they encountered weeks of rainy weather—disaster for an outdoor show. The situation grew worse when a steamboat sunk in the Mississippi River with their equipment and livestock. By the end of the winter, the show had lost $60,000.

There was one bright spot on the tour. Toward the end of the season, Cody hired a pretty young woman who could outshoot any man in the world—including Buffalo Bill himself. Her stage name was Annie Oakley, and she became one of the most popular acts of the Wild West show for many years. In June, Cody added another great attraction: Chief Sitting Bull, the most famous Indian in America. Sitting Bull quit after one season, but he brought great publicity to the show.

During the summer of 1885, the Wild West show toured Canada with great success, earning $100,000 in profits. Cody and Salsbury decided to try a new concept. Instead of traveling from town to town, they would set up in one arena for an extended run. The following summer they performed at a resort on Staten Island, New York, playing to almost 1 million people. That winter they took the show indoors to Madison Square Garden in New York City, where they played to another million people. Many western celebrities praised the show for its authenticity. Mark Twain wrote, "Down to its smallest details, the show is genuine—cowboys, vaqueros [Mexican cowboys], Indians, stage coach, costumes and all."

In 1887, Cody and Salsbury brought the authentic Wild West to England. They sailed from New York with over 200 people, including 97 Indians. There were 180 horses, 18 buffalo, elk, steers, mules, donkeys, and deer. After a two-week voyage, they established headquarters at Earl's Court arena in London. The show was a huge success, playing to 30,000 people a day for six months. Cody himself was almost as popular as the show. An American entertainer who was also in London later wrote, "Bill always seemed to know exactly what to do and say . . . He fills a full-dress suit as gracefully as he does the hunter's buckskins."

After a year in England, the company returned to America and played another long run on Staten Island. The following spring, the Wild West show began a four-year tour of Europe. They were received enthusiastically in France, Italy, Austria, and Germany, but there were problems in Spain. The ringmaster and four Indians died in a flu and smallpox epidemic; seven other Indians grew sick and returned to America. By the time they reached Germany, there were rumors that the Indians were being treated poorly. Cody decided to take all of the Indians home and discuss the situation with the commissioner of Indian Affairs.

When he arrived in America, Cody received a telegram from General Nelson Miles requesting his help with Sitting Bull. A religious movement called the Ghost Dance was spreading from reservation to reservation. The agent at the Standing Rock Reservation, James McLaughlin, was concerned that Sitting Bull was using the movement to stir up resistance among the Sioux. General Miles wanted Cody to speak to Sitting Bull and convince him to talk peacefully with Miles. If that failed, Miles gave Cody the authority to arrest his former friend and star performer.

When Cody arrived on the reservation, McLaughlin insisted on handling the situation with his Indian police—a hand-picked force of Sioux who helped control the other Indians on the reservation. On December 15, 1890, Sitting Bull was killed in a confrontation between his followers and McLaughlin's police. His death provoked a violent outbreak among the Sioux that led to the massacre at Wounded Knee on December 29. In mid-January, when the last of the Indians surrendered, they offered 19 of their leaders as hostages. Ironically, these hostages were "punished" by being turned over to Cody as performers in the Wild West show. Obviously, the commissioner of Indian Affairs found no fault with Cody's treatment of the Indians.

The spectacular battle scene of Buffalo Bill's Wild West show. Omaha, Nebraska, around 1906.
(Wyoming State Museum)

Buffalo Bill

While Cody was back in America, Nate Salsbury developed his old idea of demonstrating horsemanship from all over the world. The show was titled: "Buffalo Bill's Wild West and Congress of Rough Riders of the World." It was the biggest show yet. Along with star performers such as Buffalo Bill and Annie Oakley, the cast included 100 Sioux Indians, 25 cowboys, 20 Mexican vaqueros, 6 cowgirls, 20 U.S. soldiers, 20 English soldiers, 20 German soldiers, 6 Argentine gauchos, and a 37-man mounted cowboy band.

After four years overseas, the show returned to America for the 1893 Columbian Exposition in Chicago. This was Cody's greatest American triumph. The show was opened by President Grover Cleveland and played to capacity crowds for six months, earning over $1 million. It was the most successful run in the history of outdoor entertainment. Although the show was not actually part of the exposition, many people who attended the Wild West show thought it *was* the exposition. They went home completely satisfied, never knowing that they had actually missed the real exposition.

After the Columbian Exposition, the Wild West show continued to tour for 20 years, but it was a long, downhill slide. In 1894 Nate Salsbury grew ill, and James Bailey of the Barnum & Bailey circus was taken on as a partner. Bailey set up a series of barnstorming tours, with the show crisscrossing the country in 52 railroad cars, making over 100 stops each season. These tours were successful financially, but Cody hated the constant travel.

Nate Salsbury died at the end of 1902, two days before the Wild West show began another grueling four-year tour of England and Europe. Although the show was still appreciated overseas, it was no longer the great sensation that it had been on its earlier visits. Toward the end of the tour, James Bailey died, leaving Cody as sole manager of the show. Unfortunately, Cody—who was a notoriously poor businessman—no longer owned the show that bore his name. In 1909 Bailey's relatives sold Buffalo Bill's Wild West to Gordon W. Lillie, who called himself "Pawnee Bill."

At first, Lillie paid the bills and allowed Cody to buy back half the show out of their profits. Finally, at the end of the 1912 season, Lillie asked his partner to split the cost of keeping the show together during the winter. Cody considered it a reasonable request; the problem was that he had no money.

Cody made millions of dollars during his lifetime, but he was extremely generous—to family, friends, and people on the street.

He had bought over 200,000 acres in northwestern Wyoming, where the town of Cody had been formed in 1896. It was a good investment, but it had not yet paid off. Another investment was not so good. Between 1902 and 1912, he had thrown half a million dollars away on a mine in Arizona.

To keep up his end of the bargain, Cody borrowed $20,000 from Harry M. Tammen, the publisher of the Denver *Post* and the owner of a small circus. Cody intended to pay off the loan from future profits, but 1913 turned out to be a terrible year, with heavy rains and small crowds. That was fine with Tammen. He didn't want the $20,000; he wanted Buffalo Bill for his own circus. When the Wild West show played Denver in July 1913, Tammen had it closed down by the sheriff and sold its livestock and supplies to pay Bill's debt. After 30 years, Buffalo Bill's Wild West no longer existed.

That fall Cody formed a movie production company and made a series of short films that depicted real western events, such as Custer's defeat, using some of the Indians and soldiers who had been there. It was a creative idea, but it made little money. Finally, he gave in to pressure from Tammen and joined his circus. Cody's only role was to ride into the ring and introduce the show. Although now in his late sixties, Buffalo Bill still looked good on a horse, and the audiences came to see a living legend. After two years with the circus, Cody joined the Miller and Arlington Wild West Show for one final tour. His last performance was November 4, 1916.

William F. Cody died on January 10, 1917, in Denver, Colorado. He was almost 71 years old. For two days his body lay in the capitol building in Denver, where over 25,000 people paid their respects. Eighteen thousand people marched behind his casket to the funeral. Five months later, when the snows had melted, Buffalo Bill was buried on Lookout Mountain overlooking Denver. Cody wanted to be buried on a mountain overlooking Cody, Wyoming. But Harry Tammen, the man who destroyed the Wild West show, wanted Buffalo Bill for Denver. And Tammen won—for the second time. But who remembers Harry Tammen? It is Buffalo Bill we remember.

After Cody's death, there were tributes from many American leaders. Former president Theodore Roosevelt called Cody "an American of Americans [who] embodied all those traits of courage, strength, and self-reliant hardihood which are vital to the well-being of the nation." General Nelson Miles said Cody was "a high-minded gentleman and a great scout. He performed a great work in the West for the pioneers and for the generations coming after them and his exploits will live forever in history."

Although Cody's contributions to the real West are undeniable, his contribution as a Wild West showman is even greater. It is hard for us to imagine, but before Buffalo Bill's Wild West show, there was no such thing as a rodeo, no western books or plays— and of course no western movies. It was Cody who saw the appeal of the Wild West and presented it to the people of America, England, and Europe. And we remember it the way Cody presented it.

One of Cody's biographers, Don Russell, pointed out that movies and television shows always portray Indians with feathered headdresses and riding ponies, even though many Indians—for example, the Apache—did not wear feathers and seldom rode horses. The reason is that Buffalo Bill hired Sioux Indians, who did wear feathered headdresses and ride ponies. Similarly, early cowboys did not wear "cowboy" hats. However, Buffalo Bill wore a ten-gallon hat in his show, so today it is the standard cowboy costume.

William F. Cody lived many lives: wagon boy, Pony Express rider, Civil War soldier, army scout, buffalo hunter, Indian fighter, actor, writer, and Wild West showman. However, Cody was also famous for a life he never led—the life of the dime novel. Between 1869 and 1932, around 1,700 Buffalo Bill novels were published, including at least 550 different stories. Most of these stories had absolutely no connection with the real life of Buffalo Bill, but that didn't matter. Buffalo Bill was more than a hero of flesh and blood. He was an idea—an idea of the Wild West.

Chronology

February 26, 1846	William F. Cody is born in Scott County, Iowa
1860	Joins Pony Express
February 1864	Enlists in the Seventh Kansas Volunteer Cavalry to fight for the Union
March 6, 1866	Marries Louisa Frederici
1867	Is hired to provide buffalo meat for the railroad
September 15, 1868	Is hired as chief of scouts for Fifth Cavalry
July 11, 1869	Fights in the Battle of Summit Springs
December 23, 1869	First installment of *Buffalo Bill, the King of the Border Men* appears in *New York Weekly*
December 18, 1872	Cody makes his stage debut in *The Scouts of the Prairie*
July 17, 1876	Kills the Cheyenne leader Yellow Hair
May 17, 1883	First performance of the Wild West show
May 11, 1887	Command performance for Queen Victoria in London, England
1889–92	First European tour
May–Oct. 1893	Six-month run at the Columbian Exposition in Chicago
1902–1906	Second European tour
July 21, 1913	Wild West show closed down for bad debts
January 10, 1917	William F. Cody dies in Denver, Colorado

Further Reading

Young Adult Books

Burt, Olive W. *Young Wayfarers of the Early West*. New York: Hawthorne, 1968. Also includes sections on Sacagawea, Jim Bridger, and Kit Carson; 191 pp.

Cody, William F. *The Adventures of Buffalo Bill*. New York: Harper, 1904. A book for young readers based on Cody's autobiography; it is doubtful that Cody actually wrote it, and it should not be taken too seriously; however, it might be interesting for young people to read about Buffalo Bill's adventures among the Indians as they were told almost a century ago; 173 pp.

Garst, Doris Shannon. *Buffalo Bill*. New York: Julian Messner Inc., 1948. A full-length biography for young adults; includes illustrations; 214 pp.

Havighurst, Walter. *Buffalo Bill's Great Wild West Show*. New York: Random House, 1957. A full-length young adult book that focuses on the Wild West show; includes illustrations; 183 pp.

Stevens, Eden Vale. *Buffalo Bill*. New York: Putnam, 1976. A short biography for young readers; 64 pp.

Adult Books

Russell, Don. *The Lives and Legends of Buffalo Bill*. Norman: University of Oklahoma Press, 1960. The most complete and accurate biography; the style is too difficult for young readers, but it's the best source for adults who want the complete story; includes a good index.

O'Neil, Paul. *The End and the Myth*. "Show Time for the West," pp.44–89. Series: The Old West. Alexandria, VA: Time-Life Books, 1979. An excellent section on Buffalo Bill and the Wild West show; the style is clear enough for younger readers; many illustrations.

Wyatt Earp: Lawman on the Edge of the Law

Wyatt Earp in 1886, five years after the Tombstone shoot-out.
(Western History Collections, University of Oklahoma Library; Rose Collection)

*W*yatt Earp walks down the dusty streets of Tombstone, a star on his chest, a white hat on his head. He stands at the entrance of the O.K. Corral with his trusty six-shooter on his hip. Inside the corral a group of dangerous desperadoes wait for him with murder on their minds. Suddenly one of the outlaws makes his move, but

44

Wyatt Earp

Wyatt Earp is too fast. In a flurry of gunfire, Marshal Earp kills the outlaws and preserves law and order on the Arizona frontier.

That's the way it happened, right? Not exactly. The streets of Tombstone were dusty, but the rest of the scene was created by books and movies and television. The real Wyatt Earp was a gambler, prospector, and part-time lawman who walked both sides of the law. The real gunfight was the deadly explosion of a conflict between two groups of people who wanted different kinds of lives. It didn't even happen at the O.K. Corral.

Does that seem disappointing? It shouldn't. The real Wyatt Earp and the real gunfight are more interesting than the stories and the legends. In fact, the life of Wyatt Earp is one of the great adventure stories of the American West.

Wyatt Earp was born March 19, 1848, in Monmouth, Illinois. He was the middle son of a large, close family. The five Earp brothers—James, Virgil, Wyatt, Morgan, and Warren—shared many adventures throughout the West, including the incidents in Tombstone. There was also an older half-brother, Newton, and a younger sister, Adelia.

When Wyatt was two years old, the family moved across the Mississippi River to Pella, Iowa. Although Wyatt's parents were originally from the South, the Earps were strong supporters of the Union during the Civil War. Newton, James, and Virgil fought in the Union army while Wyatt and his younger brother worked on the family farm.

In the spring of 1864, Wyatt's father, Nicholas Earp, led a train of 40 covered wagons on the long trail to California. Sixteen-year-old Wyatt did a man's job: driving one of the wagons, caring for the livestock, and hunting for food along the way. The Earps settled near San Bernardino, where Wyatt became a driver for stagecoaches and freight wagons.

After four years in California, the Earps returned to the Midwest and settled in Lamar, Missouri. Wyatt and Virgil stopped along the way to work on the Union Pacific Railroad in Wyoming. The following year they caught up with their family in Lamar. On January 10, 1870, Wyatt married Urilla Sullivan. Looking for steady employment, the newlywed defeated his oldest brother Newton in an election for town constable. It appears that Wyatt did a good job in his first effort as a law officer. However, later that year his wife died in childbirth along with their unborn child.

The death of his wife seems to have been a turning point in the life of Wyatt Earp. He left Lamar and headed west toward the open frontier. In May 1871, he was arrested for stealing horses in Indian Territory but escaped to Kansas without a trial. For the next year or two, he worked as a buffalo hunter, killing the animals for their hides.

On April 21, 1875, Earp was hired as a policeman in Wichita, Kansas, under Marshal Michael Meagher. Wichita was a wild "cowtown," where thirsty cowboys drank, gambled and let off steam after driving their cattle from Texas to the railroad lines of Kansas. Earp was apparently successful at keeping the peace, but he was not the ideal public servant. At one point he was warned to turn in the fines he had collected or else he would not be paid. In the spring of 1865, he got into a fistfight with Meagher's opponent in the election for town marshal. Meahger won the election, but Wyatt Earp was fired.

Earp was probably not too concerned about losing his job. By 1876 the cattle business was dying out in Wichita, and the once-wild town was becoming quiet and respectable. The next great cowtown was Dodge City, and Wyatt Earp moved where the money was. In May 1876, Earp joined the Dodge City police force. The force also included Bat Masterson, who became Earp's life-long friend. In the evenings Earp tripled his income as a lawman by dealing cards at the Long Branch Saloon, the biggest gambling establishment in Dodge.

In the spring of 1877, Wyatt and his younger brother Morgan left Dodge for the Black Hills gold rush. It was Wyatt's first taste of "gold fever." That summer Earp traveled the Texas gambling circuit, where professional gamblers moved from town to town, taking money from the cowboys. By this time Earp was an excellent gambler. According to some stories, he was an excellent cheater; others say he was honest and intelligent. In either case, he was usually a winner, and gambling was his main source of income for much of his life.

While traveling through Texas, Earp met Doc Holliday, the famous gambling dentist who became feared throughout the West as a ruthless gunman. Holliday was dying of tuberculosis. He was a dangerous killer because he drank too much and didn't care whether he lived or died. Earp was a careful man who drank very little, but he and Holliday quickly became close friends. It was a friendship that proved costly in the end.

Earp and Holliday returned to Dodge City in May of 1878, and Wyatt became assistant marshal. That summer, on July 28, Earp and another officer exchanged shots with a group of drunken cowboys. One of the cowboys fell off his horse with a wound in his arm and died four weeks later. He was probably the first man Wyatt Earp killed—and the only man he killed in Dodge.

Legends about Dodge City lawmen began to grow while Earp was still serving on the police force. A writer named Ned Buntline wrote wild, fictional stories—called dime novels—with Earp and the other lawmen as heroes. Earp apparently allowed people to believe these legends and would sometimes exaggerate his own exploits. He felt it gave him an edge in a fight if the other man thought Wyatt Earp was the fastest gunfighter in the West.

In September 1879, Earp left Dodge City with his second wife, Celia Ann (Mattie) Blaylock. There is no record of when they met or if they were officially married, but they had probably been together for a number of years. The Earps were accompanied by Wyatt's older brother James, his wife, and Doc Holliday. The group picked up Virgil Earp and his wife along the way; Morgan would meet them in a few days. The Earp brothers were going to Tombstone.

In 1877, silver had been discovered about 70 miles southeast of Tucson. By early 1879 the town of Tombstone had begun to form in the dusty desert near the mines. When the Earps arrived in December, it was a collection of tents and ramshackle buildings with a population of 1,000. Within a year Tombstone was a bustling city of almost 10,000, the largest in the Arizona Territory.

The Earp brothers had big plans for Tombstone. James, Virgil, and Wyatt considered themselves businessmen, and they saw the booming city as an opportunity to make their fortunes. They bought real estate and filed mining claims. At first Wyatt rode shotgun for Wells Fargo—a freighting and banking company that transported gold, silver, and currency. Later Wyatt became part owner of a large drinking and gambling establishment called the Oriental Saloon. James worked as a bartender. Virgil was a deputy U.S. marshal. There was no salary connected with the job, but it allowed Virgil to wear a gun legally in town. Tombstone was one of the wildest boomtowns on the frontier. It was a good idea to be on the right side of a gun.

In July 1880, Wyatt was appointed deputy sheriff for the Tombstone District of Pima County. Morgan took over Wyatt's job with Wells Fargo. Warren, the youngest of the Earp boys, also arrived. The five Earp brothers were tall, handsome men with thick mustaches. They looked alike and they often dressed alike, with long black coats, black Stetson hats, white shirts, and black string ties. They were a family that stuck together, and friends like Doc Holliday and Bat Masterson stuck with them. Two of the Earps were lawmen, and they were slowly gaining power in Tombstone. It was only natural that they'd rub a few people the wrong way.

The Clantons were also a family that stuck together. There were three sons—Ike, Phin, and Billy. Their father, "Old Man" Clanton, was the leader of a gang of cowboys who lived on ranches outside of Tombstone. The Clanton gang specialized in rustling cattle from Mexico. Like the Earps, the Clantons had friends who stuck with them. They included the McLaury brothers, Frank and Tom, as well as the well-known outlaws Curly Bill Brocius and John Ringo.

The Earps and the Clantons represented two opposing forces that clashed throughout the Wild West. The Earps were businessmen who lived in town. For them, the law was a way to control the situation. A peaceful town was good for business. The Clantons were cowboys, men who lived in the wide open spaces. They were on the land long before Tombstone existed. They saw the Earps and the other townspeople as newcomers who were trying to control their free and easy life-style.

The trouble between the Earps and the Clantons began in October 1880, when Curly Bill Brocius killed the Tombstone town marshal, Fred White. As deputy county sheriff, Wyatt captured the outlaw at the scene and knocked him cold with the barrel of his gun. Before he died, Marshal White said that the shooting was accidental, so Curly Bill was released. Virgil Earp was appointed town marshal.

In early 1881, a new county—called Cochise County—was formed around Tombstone. Wyatt hoped to become county sheriff, a well-paid position with a salary and many fees. Controlling the sheriff's office would be a big step for the Earp family. However, the Arizona governor appointed another deputy sheriff named Johnny Behan. This added fuel to the fires that were smoldering in Tombstone.

Like most of the cowboys, Behan was a southern Democrat. The Earps were Republicans and former Union men. Behan was sympathetic to the Clanton gang and was probably taking bribes from them. The Earps wanted the Clantons run out of the county. Although Behan was the chief lawman in the county, Virgil Earp, as town marshal, enforced the law in Tombstone. To make matters worse, Johnny Behan and Wyatt Earp both fell in love with the same woman, a dark-eyed beauty named Josephine Marcus. She chose Wyatt Earp.

In March 1881, a stagecoach carrying a Wells Fargo payroll was robbed outside of Tombstone and two men were killed. By this time Wyatt Earp had been appointed a deputy U.S. marshal. He arrested a man who identified three members of the Clanton gang as being involved in the holdup. Sheriff Behan apparently allowed the witness to escape from the county jail. Earp then made a secret deal with Ike Clanton to betray his fellow gang members. Clanton could have the reward money; Earp only wanted the public recognition to help him defeat Johnny Behan in the next election. However, before Clanton could betray them, the three holdup men were killed. Ike Clanton got very nervous.

In June 1881, Johnny Behan arrested Doc Holliday for the robbery. This was an attempt by Behan to turn suspicion away from himself and the Clanton gang and place it on the Earps. Holliday was released, but rumors began to circulate that it was actually the Earps who robbed the stage, using Morgan's inside information about Wells Fargo. A war of words began, with the town of Tombstone split down the middle.

In September, Virgil Earp arrested two men for another stage robbery. One was Johnny Behan's deputy; the other was a friend of the Clantons. Around the same time, Ike Clanton got the idea that Wyatt had "spilled the beans" about their deal. The two sides moved quickly toward a showdown.

On the night of October 25, 1881, Ike Clanton came into town for an all-night bout of drinking and gambling. He got into a shouting match with Doc Holliday and Morgan Earp, who were just as drunk and hotheaded as he was. The next morning Clanton was armed with a six-shooter and a rifle. Virgil Earp arrested him for carrying a gun in town, smashing him on the side of the head with his six-shooter as he hauled him off to court. In the courtroom Wyatt and Morgan exchanged threats with Clanton, who was fined $25 and released. As he was leaving, Wyatt ran into Tom McLaury, who was coming to bail out Clanton. They exchanged more threats, and Wyatt smashed McLaury across the skull with his revolver.

During the next hour, Billy Clanton and Frank McLaury joined their brothers in town. One of the townspeople notified Sheriff Johnny Behan and Marshal Virgil Earp that it looked like the cowboys were getting ready for trouble. Behan went to disarm them. Ike Clanton and Tom McLaury were not armed, but Billy Clanton and Frank McLaury refused to give up their guns unless Behan also disarmed the Earps.

As Behan walked away from the cowboys, he confronted Virgil Earp, who was accompanied by Wyatt, Morgan, and Doc Holliday. the Earps and Holliday brushed past the sheriff and walked toward the Clantons and the McLaurys. The cowboys stood in a vacant lot between a house and a photograph gallery. The back entrance of the O.K. Corral was located a few doors down.

Virgil approached the cowboys with Wyatt and Morgan behind him and Doc bringing up the rear. The two groups were six feet apart. Virgil carried Doc's cane in his right hand. He obviously wasn't expecting a fight. But just in case, Doc carried a sawed-off shotgun under his long gray gambler's coat. The cowboys could see it clearly as the coat flapped in the desert wind.

"Give up your arms or throw up your arms," Virgil ordered.

What happened next is lost in history. Some witnesses said that Billy Clanton and Frank McLaury cocked their guns. Others said that the cowboys were about to surrender their guns. One eyewitness said that Frank McLaury and Doc Holliday shot simultaneously. Others said that the first shots were fired by Doc Holliday and Morgan Earp, who were probably full of whiskey.

Whoever fired first, the vacant lot exploded with gunfire. It lasted less than a minute. When it was over, Billy Clanton and the McLaury brothers were dead or dying. Ike Clanton ran away when the shooting started. Virgil and Morgan Earp were seriously wounded. Doc Holliday had a flesh wound. Wyatt Earp walked away without a scratch.

The next day one of the Tombstone newspapers quoted an eyewitness as saying, "Wyatt Earp stood up and fired in rapid succession, as cool as a cucumber, and was not hit. Doc Holliday was as calm as if at target practice, and fired rapidly."

Johnny Behan arrested Wyatt Earp and Doc Holliday on charges of murder. Virgil was suspended as town marshal. The murder trial lasted 30 days, with the entire town taking sides. Virgil Earp testified that he had deputized Doc Holliday on the spot and that Wyatt Earp was helping him as a deputy U.S. marshal. Morgan Earp was already serving as a special policeman.

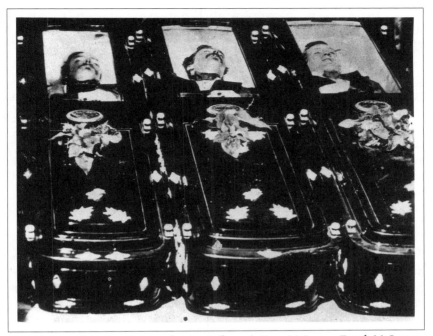

The victims of the Tombstone shoot-out (l. to r.): Tom McLaury, Frank McLaury, Billy Clanton. Their silver-trimmed caskets were displayed in the window of a hardware store, and a brass band accompanied them to the cemetery.
(Arizona Historical Society/Tucson)

Judge Wells Spicer criticized Virgil Earp for asking Wyatt and Doc Holliday to help him. However, he ruled that the Earps and Holliday "were officers charged with the duty of arresting and disarming brave and determined men who were experts in the use of firearms, as quick as thought and as certain as death, and who had previously declared their intentions not to be arrested nor disarmed . . . it was a necessary act done in the discharge of official duty."

The verdict did not satisfy the cowboys and their supporters. On the night of December 28, two months after the shooting, Virgil Earp was ambushed while crossing the street. His left arm was shattered and remained useless for the rest of his life. Three months later, Morgan Earp was murdered while playing pool. Several friends of the Clantons were seen nearby.

Now Wyatt Earp took the law into his own hands. He sent Virgil, along with Morgan's body, to their parents' home in California. Wyatt, Doc Holliday, Warren Earp, and two other friends accompanied the train as far as Tucson. At the station they spotted Frank Stilwell, one of the men suspected in Morgan's murder. The next morning Stilwell's body was found riddled with buckshot and bullets.

The group then returned to Tombstone and set off as a posse in search of the other men suspected in Morgan's death. Wyatt Earp was still a deputy U.S. marshal, and he claimed to have legal warrants. On the way out of town, Johnny Behan tried to arrest Earp for Stilwell's murder, but Earp just rode past him. Behan organized his own posse and went after him.

The next morning the Earp posse killed another suspect named Florentino Cruz. A few days later Earp apparently killed Curly Bill Brocius, who had become a leader of the Clanton gang. By this time Johnny Behan had warrants for the murders of Frank Stilwell and Florentino Cruz. The Earp posse rode out of Arizona into New Mexico and on to Colorado. Their Tombstone days were over.

Wyatt Earp stayed for a while in the mining towns of Colorado. According to some stories, he secretly returned to Arizona and killed John Ringo, the last of the Clanton leaders. He then visited San Francisco and met up with Josephine Marcus, the dark-eyed beauty who had once been Johnny Behan's girl. Although there is no record of an official marriage, Josephine later insisted that they were married on a ship off the California Coast. With or without a license, Wyatt and Josephine lived as man and wife for over 45 years. He evidently deserted his second wife, Mattie.

In 1883 Earp, Holliday, Bat Masterson and a number of other gunfighters returned to Dodge City to help Luke Short, a gambling friend who was having trouble with some business rivals. Without firing a shot, the gunfighters convinced Short's rivals to settle their problems. A Dodge City newspaper story described Wyatt Earp as "famous in the cheerful business of depopulating the country. He has killed within our personal knowledge six men, and he is popularly credited with relegating to the dust no less than ten of his fellow men."

After the Dodge City trip, Wyatt Earp tried to leave his reputation behind. He was 35 years old, newly married, and eager to make the fortune he had originally hoped to find in Tombstone. After prospecting, saloon-keeping, and gambling throughout the

The "Dodge City Peace Commissioners," 1883. In fact, they were a group of gunmen who helped an old friend with some business problems
Front row (l. to r.): Charles Bassett, Wyatt Earp, L. McLean, Neal Brown.
Back row (l. to r.): W. H. Harris, Luke Short, Bat Masterson.
(National Archives. Photograph by Camillus S. Fly)

West, he and Josephine settled down in San Diego. There Wyatt ran a gambling hall, bought real estate, and owned a small stable of race horses.

In 1896 Wyatt was asked to referee a heavyweight boxing match in San Francisco between Bob Fitzsimmons and Tom Sharkey. There was heavy betting on the fight, and Earp was chosen because of his reputation for fearless honesty. However, his honesty was questioned when he called a foul on Fitzsimmons and awarded the decision to Sharkey, who was the underdog. At the age of 48, Wyatt Earp was back in the middle of controversy. The official investigation found no wrongdoing, but Earp was fined $50 for carrying a concealed weapon into the ring. It was an old six-shooter from his days on the frontier.

A few months after the fight, Earp was once again infected with gold fever when he heard of the rich finds in the Klondike region of Canada. Although Wyatt and Josephine traveled up the Yukon River toward the Klondike, they never reached the goldfields. Instead Earp and a partner built an elegant and successful saloon in Nome, Alaska. Earp sold his interest in 1902.

In 1906, after years of prospecting, Wyatt and Josephine Earp finally discovered a gold mine in the Mojave Desert of Southern California. It never produced the riches they had dreamed of, but it did provide them with a small income. They built a house near the mine and spent their winters there for more than 20 years.

During the summers the Earps lived in Los Angeles. Wyatt became friends with cowboy stars William S. Hart and Tom Mix and served as an unpaid advisor for western films. In 1928, at the age of 80, Earp met a writer named Stuart Lake. The two men began to work on a book about Earp's life, but Earp never saw the finished product. On January 13, 1929, Wyatt Earp died in his Los Angeles home.

In his *Encyclopedia of Western Gunfighters*, Bill O'Neal writes, "Because of highly conflicting versions of his career, no individual has caused greater controversy in western history than Wyatt Earp." The controversy began during Earp's life, but it continues to haunt him after death. Part of the blame must be placed on Stuart Lake.

Two years after Earp's death, Lake's book, *Wyatt Earp: Frontier Marshal*, was published. It was an immediate success. Lake was an excellent writer who knew how to tell a good story. He portrayed Earp as a saintly hero who preserved law and order on the western frontier. It was a wonderful tale, and it became the inspiration for movies and television shows.

Lake wrote as if the entire story had been dictated by Earp himself. Actually, Wyatt Earp never saw the manuscript of the book, and it is doubtful that he would have approved of it.

Wyatt Earp

Although Earp exaggerated some of his adventures during his life, he apparently wanted to set the record straight before he died.

The Lake book created a strong anti-Earp feeling among some historians and western writers. They felt that Earp had lied about his past in order to create a heroic image. New books appeared in which Wyatt Earp was portrayed as a common criminal and a cold-blooded killer.

In fact, Wyatt Earp was probably somewhere between the extremes of hero and criminal. He was a tough, brave man of the frontier. He enforced the law when it served his purposes and took the law into his own hands when he felt it was necessary. He traveled the west from Texas to Alaska in search of riches. Although he never found the wealth he dreamed of, he lived a life of excitement and adventure that was more valuable than gold.

In his long life, Wyatt Earp was a stagecoach driver, railroad worker, buffalo hunter, gambler, lawman, prospector, horse racer, and saloon-keeper. Perhaps the fairest assessment is simply this: Wyatt Earp was a man of the Wild West.

Chronology

March 19, 1848	Wyatt Earp is born in Monmouth, Illinois
January 10, 1870	Marries Urilla Sullivan; she dies that year
May 1871	Is arrested for stealing horses in Indian Territory
April 21, 1875	Is hired as a policeman in Wichita, Kansas
May 1876	Is hired as a policeman in Dodge City, Kansas
December 1879	The Earps arrive in Tombstone, Arizona
October 1880	Tombstone marshal Fred White is killed
March 16, 1881	Stagecoach carrying Wells Fargo payroll is robbed: two men are killed
June 1881	Sheriff Behan arrests Doc Holliday
September 1881	Virgil Earp arrests two Clanton supporters for second stagecoach robbery
October 26, 1881	Shootout between the Earps and the Clantons
December 1, 1881	Judge Spicer finds the Earps and Holliday not guilty
December 28, 1881	Virgil Earp is ambushed; his left arm shattered
March 1882	Morgan Earp is killed; Wyatt Earp kills three Clanton gang members and leaves Arizona
Spring 1883	Earp and friends form "Dodge City Peace Commission" to help Luke Short
December 2, 1896	Earp serves as referee for a heavyweight boxing championship in San Francisco
January 13, 1929	Wyatt Earp dies in Los Angeles

Further Reading

Young Adult Books

Holbrook, Stewart Hall. *Wyatt Earp, U.S. Marshal.* Landmark Books, volume 67. New York: Random House, 1956. A full-length young adult biography; as the title suggests, it accepts the erroneous concept of Earp as a frontier marshal; includes illustrations; 180 pp.

Lake, Stuart N. *The Life and Times of Wyatt Earp.* Boston: Houghton Mifflin Co., 1956. A shortened version of Lake's famous book, *Wyatt Earp: Frontier Marshal*; although many of Lake's scenes are pure fiction, young readers might be interested in reading the book that created many of the legends; includes illustrations; 271 pp.

Adult Books

Earp, Josephine Sarah Marcus. *I Married Wyatt Earp: The Recollections of Josephine Sarah Marcus Earp,* collected and edited by Glenn G. Boyer. Tucson: University of Arizona Press, 1976. This is really two books; Mrs. Earp's manuscript is obviously "pro-Earp," but it sheds interesting light on Earp's character; the notes by Boyer are extensive and provide an extremely accurate balance to Mrs. Earp's rosy point of view; the manuscript is easy to read but the notes are somewhat complicated.

O'Neal, Bill. *Encyclopedia of Western Gunfighters,* pp. 96–103. Norman: University of Oklahoma Press, 1979. Anti-Earp but interesting; also includes entries on Morgan, Virgil, and Warren Earp as well as many other famous gunmen; the entries are short and the style is fairly clear.

Trachtman, Paul. *The Gunfighters.* "An epic showdown at the O.K. Corral," pp. 15–37. Series: The Old West. Alexandria, VA: Time-Life Books, 1974. An accurate, even-handed account of the Tombstone conflict; clear enough for most young readers.

Billy the Kid:
A Violent Boy in
a Violent World

Billy the Kid. The original photograph was a tintype in which the image is reversed. Although Billy's six-shooter appears to be on his left hip, he was actually right-handed and wore his gun on his right hip. The tintype created a legend that Billy was left-handed, a typical example of how legends were formed in the Wild West.
(National Archives)

---

*B*illy the Kid stood on the balcony of the Lincoln County Courthouse, an empty shotgun in his hands, his broken leg irons tucked into his belt. He had just fired both barrels of the shotgun into a deputy in the yard below. Another deputy lay dead behind the courthouse. The citizens of Lincoln gazed up at the 21-year-old outlaw in a combination of wonder and fear. Some wanted him dead; some were happy to see him free. A few young ladies were in love with him. No one made a move. An hour later, carrying a small arsenal of weapons, he calmly rode out of town.

This is one of the most famous moments in the career of the outlaw known as Billy the Kid. Along with Jesse James, the Kid rides in the first rank of Wild West outlaws. But unlike the serious, self-righteous Jesse, Billy was a happy-go-lucky young man who seemed to think all the killing was part of a wonderful adventure. Perhaps the most unusual aspect of the Kid's career as an outlaw was that people liked him.

The early life of Billy the Kid remains a mystery. Even his name and the date of his birth are uncertain. Most authorities believe his real name was Henry McCarty; others think it was William H. Bonney, the name he used in later life. He was probably born in New York City during the last few months of 1859. His mother was Catherine McCarty, and he had a brother named Joe. The identity of his father is unknown.

On March 1, 1873, Catherine McCarty and William Antrim were married in Santa Fe, New Mexico, with Henry and Joe acting as witnesses. This is the first official proof of the future outlaw's existence. After the wedding the Antrim family moved to Silver City, a boomtown in southwestern New Mexico. On September 16, 1874, Catherine died of tuberculosis. Although William Antrim was a good, hard-working man, he offered little or no supervision to his two stepsons.

In September 1875, Henry and an older boy stole some clothes from a Chinese laundry as a joke. When Henry got caught with the stolen goods, the sheriff locked the 15-year-old in jail to teach him a lesson. After two days Henry climbed up the jailhouse chimney and escaped. It was the first of many escapes for the boy who became Billy the Kid.

In Henry's mind, the theft and escape probably seemed more serious than they really were. He left New Mexico and went to Arizona, where he worked on a ranch and was later arrested for stealing horses. He began using his stepfather's name, calling himself Henry Antrim, William Antrim, or Kid Antrim. Older men just called him "the Kid."

Although he seldom drank, the Kid enjoyed hanging out in saloons, where he would gamble and socialize. On the night of August 17, 1877, a drunken bully named Windy Cahill began to taunt the Kid. The man and the boy pounced on each other and rolled around on the barroom floor. In the scuffle, the Kid pulled out his pistol and shot Cahill in the belly. Windy Cahill died the next day.

Considering the situation—as well as the violent nature of the Wild West—it is likely that the killing would have been considered self-defense. But the Kid didn't wait around to find out. He broke out of the Camp Grant guardhouse and headed back to New Mexico.

Two years earlier, Henry McCarty had left New Mexico as a frightened boy of 15. He returned as Kid Antrim—a "man" of 17. He was still boyish looking, with a smooth, pleasant face accentuated by intense blue eyes and two buck teeth. He stood five foot seven inches tall and weighed perhaps 135 pounds. But despite his small size, he had begun to develop the toughness and self-confidence that continued to grow throughout his short life. He knew how to use a gun, and he had killed a man. He had also learned to speak Spanish fluently, which made him very popular among the Hispanic people.

In September 1877, the Kid apparently joined a band of outlaws under Jesse Evans. The gang stole some horses in the Silver City area—the Kid's old hometown—and then rode across southern New Mexico, stopping at saloons and helping themselves to food and drink. It was around this time that Henry McCarty, alias Kid Antrim, began to use the name William H. Bonney.

The end of the trail for the Evans gang was Lincoln County, a wide-open cattle range in the southwest corner of New Mexico. Without realizing it, the Kid was being drawn into a bloody conflict that became known as the Lincoln County War.

On its simplest level, the conflict was between two groups of greedy men who wanted to control the economy of the county. On one side was The House, a large general store owned by James Dolan and John Riley. Most of the ranchers, farmers, and sheepherders were in debt to The House. Dolan employed rustlers such as Jesse Evans to supply him with cheap beef, which he then sold to the government for army posts and Indian reservations. The House was supported by a corrupt group of politicians in Santa Fe as well as by the county sheriff, William Brady.

On the other side were a wealthy English rancher named John Tunstall and a lawyer named Alexander McSween. Before Billy arrived, Tunstall and McSween had established a store and bank in direct competition with The House. They were supported by a powerful rancher named John Chisum, who competed with The House for government beef contracts.

In December 1877, Billy was hired by John Tunstall's foreman, Dick Brewer. Although he was supposedly hired to work on the Tunstall ranch, Brewer was actually putting together a group of gunmen in case the conflict with The House exploded in violence. About two months later, on February 18, 1878, John Tunstall was riding into Lincoln with some of his men, including the Kid. Toward dusk, he was ambushed and killed by three men from a posse organized by Sheriff Brady. Tunstall's death had a profound effect on the Kid, who swore he would get revenge. The death also had a profound effect on the Territory of New Mexico: the Lincoln County War had begun.

Alexander McSween obtained a warrant for the arrest of the entire posse involved in Tunstall's murder. Dick Brewer formed Tunstall's supporters into a group called the Regulators, which claimed to be a legal posse formed to serve the warrant. Brady, Dolan, and their men also claimed to be on the side of the law because they held an arrest warrant for McSween and a legal order to confiscate his property. These legal papers were related to an earlier charge of embezzlement against McSween.

In early March, the Regulators executed two of the men wanted in the murder of John Tunstall and killed another man who objected to the execution. Billy participated in all three murders. On April 1, Billy and five other men ambushed Sheriff Brady as he was walking down the main street of Lincoln with his deputies. Brady and one deputy were killed. The murder of the county sheriff turned public opinion against the Regulators.

The Regulators' image grew worse on April 4. At Blazer's Mills, a small settlement located within the Mescalero Indian Reservation, 14 Regulators engaged in a bloody shootout with a Dolan supporter named Buckshot Roberts. When the shooting was over, Roberts and Dick Brewer were dead. Although he was later blamed for it, Billy did not kill Roberts.

A week later Billy and his companions were indicted in the murder of Sheriff Brady. In June a federal warrant was issued for Billy and the other Regulators involved in Buckshot Roberts' death. The killing was considered a federal crime because it took place on an Indian reservation. Thus Billy was now wanted by the U.S. government for the murder of Roberts and by the Territory of New Mexico for the murder of Sheriff Brady.

On the night of July 14, Alexander McSween and 60 Regulators rode into Lincoln and took up defensive positions throughout the town. The following afternoon Dolan's posse rode into town with 40 men. This became the famous "Five-Day Battle of Lincoln."

For the first four days, the two sides jockeyed for position. Although the Regulators outnumbered Dolan's men, they were weakened by being divided into three groups, located in three separate buildings. On the morning of July 19, Lieutenant Colonel Nathan Dudley arrived from Fort Stanton with 4 officers, 35 soldiers, a howitzer (a small cannon), and a Gatling gun (an early machine gun). Dudley claimed to be neutral, but he pointed his guns directly at two of the Regulators' strongholds. The men ran for the nearby hills, leaving the remaining group in Alexander McSween's house to face the Dolan posse alone.

That afternoon the soldiers watched as Dolan's men set the McSween house on fire. It was an adobe structure, and the flames grew slowly through the afternoon and evening. At 9:00 P.M. Billy Bonney led four other men in a daring escape out the back door. One man was killed, but Billy and three companions made it safely into the hills. Shortly afterward McSween and the other men emerged from the house. In a violent shootout, McSween and three others were killed.

The Battle of Lincoln was over. Tunstall and McSween were dead. The Dolan store was bankrupt. There was no reason to continue fighting. But Billy and some of the other Regulators refused to quit. In August, there was another battle on the Mescalero reservation in which a government clerk was killed. The following month Billy and four others stole 15 horses from a Dolan supporter and sold them in the Texas panhandle. This began a new "career" for Billy as a horse and cattle rustler.

In February 1879, Billy returned to Lincoln and met with Dolan and his men. The two sides made peace and agreed not to testify against each other. Afterward they celebrated by getting drunk—except Billy, who went along but didn't drink. That night one of the drunken Dolan men shot and killed a lawyer named Huston Chapman. Billy and a friend, Tom O'Folliard, both witnessed the shooting. Shortly afterward they slipped away and left town.

In early March, the new governor of New Mexico, Lew Wallace, arrived in Lincoln. Wallace had issued a general amnesty to the men who took part in the Lincoln County War. However, the amnesty did not apply to Billy because he was under indictment for two murders. Now Wallace wanted to put an end to the fighting once and for all. He was especially interested in finding the killer of Huston Chapman, because that murder took place after the amnesty.

Billy wrote a note to Wallace indicating that he would testify in the Chapman murder if the governor would pardon him on his own murder charges. Wallace agreed. On the night of March 17, the outlaw and the governor met secretly and formed a plan in which Billy would be arrested for his own protection. In April, Billy and Tom O'Folliard testified in the Chapman murder case. Although Billy had done his part, the district attorney was a strong Dolan supporter and refused to drop the murder charges, as Wallace had promised. Knowing of the governor's promise, the Lincoln County sheriff, George Kimball, allowed Billy and Tom to escape in mid-June.

For the rest of his life, Billy spent most of his time in and around Fort Sumner—a small settlement along the Pecos River about 100 miles northeast of Lincoln. It had originally been an army fort, but now the military buildings served as homes, stores and saloons. With his fluent Spanish, Billy was very popular among the Hispanic people of the town, especially the pretty senoritas. Billy also found many outlaw friends in the area, who accompanied him on horse- and cattle-rustling raids.

Although he was wanted on two murder charges, Billy was not yet a notorious outlaw. Beginning in January 1880, however, a series of events made William H. Bonney famous in New Mexico.

The first occurred in a Fort Sumner saloon, where Billy gunned down a drunk named Joe Grant. Although the killing was considered self-defense, an eyewitness reported that Bonney calmly put three bullets in Grant's chin—all within a space no larger than a half dollar. This added to Billy's reputation as a gunman.

Around this time Billy began a public feud with cattleman John Chisum. Billy claimed that Chisum owed him $500 for his services during the Lincoln County War. Chisum denied ever promising to pay Tunstall's men. Because Chisum was famous, the feud placed Billy in the public eye.

On October 16, 1880, the U.S. mail was robbed as it left Fort Stanton. Billy was identified among the robbers. At the same time, he was suspected in connection with a counterfeiting ring operating out of White Oaks, a mining town about 30 miles northwest of Lincoln. Suddenly Billy Bonney was a big-time outlaw.

On November 27, 1880, a posse surrounded Billy and two other rustlers in a house outside of White Oaks. Hostages were exchanged during the seven-hour standoff. Finally, the outlaws' hostage was killed, apparently murdered by Billy and his two companions. The posse backed down and the outlaws escaped, but this killing established Billy as a hardened criminal.

Pat Garrett. As sheriff of Lincoln County, he captured
Billy the Kid and brought him to justice;
when the Kid escaped Garrett killed him.
(National Archives)

Billy the Kid

On December 3, the newspaper in Las Vegas, New Mexico, referred to "Billy the Kid" as the leader of a huge outlaw gang. Although it wasn't true, newspapers across the country repeated the story. Ten days later Governor Lew Wallace—the man who had once promised to pardon Billy—set a $500 reward for the capture of "Bonney alias 'the Kid.' " Billy the Kid was now the most wanted outlaw in the Southwest.

By this time there was a new sheriff in Lincoln County. Pat Garrett was a tall, tough, former buffalo hunter. As a bartender in Fort Sumner, he had become acquainted with Billy, but stories of a deep friendship are exaggerated. On the night of December 19, Garrett and 18 men ambushed the Kid and five companions as they rode into Fort Sumner. Tom O'Folliard was killed, but Billy and the others escaped.

Four nights later, Garrett and his men surrounded the outlaws in an old stone house at Stinking Springs, east of Fort Sumner. At dawn one of Billy's companions, Charley Bowdre, came out to feed his horse. Garrett's men killed Bowdre and then killed his horse, thus blocking the doorway. All day Billy and the others waited inside, cold and hungry. When Garrett's men began to cook their dinner in the late afternoon, the outlaws surrendered. Billy later said, "We could have stayed in the house, but . . . they would have starved us out. I though it was better to come out and get a good square meal."

Garrett took the prisoners on a wagon to Las Vegas and then on a train to Santa Fe, where they were locked in the jailhouse. In both towns, large crowds came out to see the notorious Billy the Kid. Billy enjoyed the attention, smiling at the onlookers and joking with newspaper reporters. "What's the use of looking on the gloomy side of everything," Billy said. "The laugh's on me this time."

On March 30, 1881, Billy appeared before the U.S. District Court in Mesilla on the federal charge of murdering Buckshot Roberts. A week later the judge dismissed the case on the grounds that Blazer's Mills—where the shooting occurred—was not on federal land. Billy then went to trial for the murder of Sheriff Brady. This time he wasn't so lucky. On April 9, the jury found him guilty of first-degree murder. He was sentenced to death by hanging in Lincoln on May 13.

There was no secure jail in Lincoln, so Billy was held in handcuffs and leg irons on the second floor of the county courthouse; ironically it was the old Dolan store building. Garrett assigned two deputies to guard the Kid. One was a fair-minded man named James Bell; the other was a Dolan supporter named Bob Olinger, who taunted the Kid with a double-barreled shotgun.

On the evening of April 28, Sheriff Garrett was out of town. When Olinger took five other prisoners across the street to eat dinner, Billy asked Bell if he could visit the outhouse. Bell agreed. On the way back, Billy got ahead of Bell and moved quickly up the stairs, slipping one hand out of the handcuff. When Bell caught up to him, Billy swung the loose cuff and knocked the deputy down the stairs. He then shot and killed him, either with Bell's gun or with a gun that had been hidden in the outhouse.

Billy went to Garrett's office, where he found Olinger's shotgun. Olinger had stepped out into the street below, alarmed by the shot that killed Bell. Billy called to him through the second-story window; when Olinger looked up, the Kid blasted him with both barrels of his own shotgun. Billy then stepped out on the balcony and spoke to the people of the town. He said he was sorry that he had to kill Bell but that Olinger deserved to die. An hour later, carrying a small arsenal of revolvers and pistols, Billy the Kid rode out of Lincoln for the last time.

Billy headed north to Fort Sumner where he had many friends who would hide him. Although there were reports of his presence in the area, Pat Garrett was hesitant to look for him there. Garrett respected the Kid's intelligence, and the smart move would have been to leave New Mexico.

Finally Garrett decided to investigate. On the night of July 14, 1881, the sheriff and two deputies went to Pete Maxwell's house in Fort Sumner. Maxwell was a friend of both Billy and Garrett. While his deputies waited outside, Garrett entered Maxwell's bedroom and sat on the edge of the bed. When Garrett asked if the Kid was in town, Maxwell was nervous and vague in his reply.

At the same time, the Kid was visiting another friend nearby, possibly a girlfriend. He wanted something to eat, and he knew that Maxwell had a freshly butchered yearling hanging on his porch. In his stocking feet, Billy walked to Maxwell's house, carrying a butcher knife in his left hand and his six-shooter in his right hand. Outside the house he was startled by Garrett's deputies. He whispered in Spanish, "Quien es? Quien es?" (Who is it?) He then backed into Maxwell's house and into the bedroom.

Inside, he asked Maxwell about the men outside. Then he noticed the dark figure sitting on the edge of the bed. *"Quien es?"* he whispered, backing away. *"Quien es?"*

Pete Maxwell's house in Fort Sumner, New Mexico. Billy the Kid was shot and killed by Pat Garrett in the first room from the left as the reader faces the photograph.
(Arizona Historical Society/Tucson)

Although he couldn't see his face, Pat Garrett recognized Billy's voice. He raised his gun and fired two shots before the Kid could respond. One of the bullets found its mark above the heart. Billy the Kid was dead at the age of 21.

In his book *Billy the Kid: A Short and Violent Life*, historian Robert M. Utley writes, "Except in its final months, the Kid's career did not measure up to its reputation. Although a superb gunman and arresting personality, he was a quite ordinary outlaw . . ." This is true. Other men were more ruthless killers. Others were more successful rustlers. And yet it is Billy the Kid who is remembered as the great outlaw of the Southwest.

Why? There are several reasons. First is Billy's connection with the Lincoln County War. Although he was just a common soldier in the bloody conflict, Billy received more than his share of the blame. Out of more than 50 men who were indicted for crimes committed during the war, Billy Bonney was the *only* one who was ever convicted. This was partly due to bad luck and partly because he drifted into more serious crimes.

Second, as Utley points out, the final months of Billy's career were extraordinary: the standoff with the posse near White Oaks, the ambush by Garrett's men in Fort Sumner, the capture in the stone house at Stinking Springs, the circus atmosphere in Las Vegas and Santa Fe, the trial in Mesilla, the daring escape in Lincoln, and the moment of truth in Pete Maxwell's darkened bedroom. No adventure writer could create a more exciting story.

Third, there is Billy's "arresting personality." He was cheerful, cocky and intelligent. At the same time, he had a quick temper that could turn violent in an instant. One friend, Dr. Henry Hoyt, described him as "a handsome youth with smooth face, wavy brown hair, an athletic and symmetrical figure, and clear blue eyes that could look one through and through. Unless angry, he always seemed to have a pleasant expression with a ready smile."

The final factor was his name—Billy the Kid. Although he was not called by this name until the last few months of his life, it appealed to editors, writers, and readers. Within one year of his death, eight books allegedly told the story of Billy the Kid. One was credited to the man who killed him: *The Authentic Life of Billy the Kid* by Pat Garrett with newspaperman Ash Upson. Despite its title, it was less than authentic.

The early stories portrayed the Kid as a vicious, cold-blooded killer. In 1926, *The Saga of Billy the Kid* by Walter Noble Burns portrayed him as a New Mexican Robin Hood who stole from the rich merchants and cattlemen in order to help the poor Hispanic people. The truth is somewhere in between. Although Billy was very popular among the Spanish-speaking people, he was no Robin Hood. Yet it is not quite fair to call him a vicious killer.

John Meadows, who knew the Kid in Lincoln, described Billy's violent nature as follows: "When he was rough, he was rough as men ever get to be . . . too awful rough at times, but everything in the country was rough about then." This seems a fair assessment. Billy the Kid was a violent young man in a violent land at a violent time. Despite his cheerful personality, he represents the dark side of the Wild West.

Chronology

c. 1859	Henry McCarty (Billy the Kid) is born in New York City
March 1, 1873	Catherine McCarty and William Antrim are married in Santa Fe, New Mexico
September 16, 1874	Catherine McCarty Antrim dies in Silver City, New Mexico
September 1875	Henry McCarty escapes up jailhouse chimney
August 17, 1877	Billy kills Windy Cahill in a barroom brawl
February 18, 1878	John Tunstall is murdered: Lincoln County War begins
April 1, 1878	Billy and five others murder Sheriff Brady
April 4, 1878	The Regulators kill Buckshot Roberts
July 15–19, 1878	Five-Day Battle of Lincoln
March 17, 1879	Billy meets with Governor Lew Wallace
January 10, 1880	Kills Joe Grant in Fort Sumner saloon
November 27, 1880	Standoff near White Oaks; one hostage killed
December 13, 1880	Governor Wallace offers $500 reward for the capture of "Bonney alias the Kid"
December 24, 1880	Billy surrenders to Pat Garrett at Stinking Springs
April 28, 1881	Escapes from the Lincoln County courthouse
July 14, 1881	Pat Garrett kills Billy the Kid in Fort Sumner

Further Reading

Young Adult Books

Ulyatt, Kenneth. *Outlaws*. New York: Harper & Row, 1978. Recommended by *Best Books for Children* for grades 6–8; includes chapters on other famous outlaws; includes illustrations.

Adult Books

Rennert, Vincent Paul. *Western Outlaws*. New York: Crowell-Collier Press, 1968. Written for adults, but a good source for younger readers; the chapter on Billy the Kid is fairly accurate; also contains chapters on Jesse James and other outlaws.

Trachtman, Paul. *The Gunfighters*, pp. 182–193. Series: The Old West. Alexandria, VA: Time-Life Books, 1974. A good, mostly accurate account written in language that young readers will understand; many illustrations.

Utley, Robert M. *Billy the Kid: A Short and Violent Life*. Lincoln: University of Nebraska Press. The most accurate full-length biography; the style is too difficult for young readers; however, it is an excellent source for adults who wish to help students in their research; contains many photographs.

Geronimo:
The Last Warrior

Geronimo. This is the earliest known photograph,
apparently taken at the San Carlos Reservation in the
spring of 1884 when Geronimo was in his late fifties.
(National Archives. Photograph by A. Frank Randall)

*T*he story of Geronimo is the story of a particular group of Apache
Indians. Geronimo's group lived in the mountains of what is now
southwestern New Mexico, southeastern Arizona, and northern
Mexico. They are often called the Chiricahua Apache, but in
Geronimo's time there were five different bands within the group;
the Chiricahua was only one of these bands. A better name for the

group would be the Southern Apache.

Geronimo's band, called the Bedonkohe, lived along the Gila River, near what is now Clifton, Arizona. Two closely related bands, the Mimbreno and Warm Springs Apache, lived to the east in New Mexico. To the south, along the Arizona-Mexican border, lived the Chiricahua band. Farther south, in the rugged Sierra Madre of Mexico, lived the Nednai.

When Geronimo was born, there were probably several thousand Apache in these five bands. They married into each other's families, helped each other in time of need, and fought together against their enemies. Although other tribes—and other Apache—fought hard and long against the white man, no group fought harder or longer than the Southern Apache. And no Apache leader fought harder or longer than Geronimo. In his final campaign, Geronimo and fewer than 20 warriors battled 5,000 U.S. troops and 4,000 Mexican soldiers for five months. When he surrendered, the wars between the United States and the American Indians were over.

Geronimo said that he was born in June of 1829, but he was probably born a few years earlier. In those days, Indians did not live by the white man's calendar. Geronimo's Apache name was Goyahkla, which means "one who yawns." His father was Taklishim, the son of a great chief named Mahko. His mother was Juana.

Chief Mahko died before Geronimo was born, and the Bedonkohe Apache did not choose another chief. Taklishim died when Geronimo was a boy. After his father's death, Geronimo and his mother went to visit the Nednai Apache in the Sierra Madre. There he became friends with Juh, who would later become chief of the Nednai and Geronimo's companion in battle.

It was probably among the Nednai that Geronimo received his final training as an Apache warrior. He learned to survive in the desert and the mountains, to travel quickly and secretly, to find the water holes, to eat his horse if necessary, to scatter if attacked and disappear into the land.

He also learned to raid and steal from the Mexicans, riding down from the Sierra Madre and attacking villages and pack trains. For an Apache warrior, this was a way of life and one of his main sources of income. The war between the Apache and the Mexicans dated back hundreds of years. There was killing and cruelty on both sides, but the Apache did not kill women and children or scalp their victims. The Mexicans offered bounties for Apache scalps: 100 pesos for the scalp of an Apache man, 50 pesos for the scalp of a woman, and 25 pesos for the scalp of a child.

Geronimo was only 17 when he was admitted to the council of warriors—a very young age by Apache standards. As a warrior, he could choose a wife, and he married a Nednai girl named Alope. With his mother and his new wife, he returned to the Bedonkohe lands near the Gila River. In time, Geronimo and Alope had three children.

Around 1850 Geronimo and his people camped in Mexico with their relatives the Mimbreno Apache. The chief of the Mimbreno was Mangas Coloradas, one of the greatest American Indian chiefs. The Bedonkohe often lived with the Mimbreno and looked to Mangas as their leader.

At this time the Mexicans and the Apache were testing a new peace. Most of the warriors, including Mangas and Geronimo, went into the towns of Janos to trade, leaving their women and children with a small guard. While they were gone, Mexican troops entered the encampment, killing 25 Apache and capturing 50. When the warriors returned, Geronimo found his mother, his wife, and his three children among the dead.

This tragedy shaped Geronimo's life. Other Apache had lost their loved ones, but no one had lost what he had lost—everything. He hated the Mexicans until the day he died. When he returned to Arizona, Geronimo heard a voice telling him that no gun or bullet would ever kill him. This was his Power, the source of his strength as a medicine man and war leader.

The next year, the five bands united and returned to Mexico to punish the troops who had massacred their women and children. In a two-hour battle outside the town of Arizpe, the Apache killed many Mexican soldiers with their spears and bows and arrows. Although he was young, Geronimo was allowed to lead the warriors because he had suffered the greatest loss. According to tradition, it was in this battle that he received the name Geronimo, the Spanish name for "Jerome."

When he returned from Arizpe, Geronimo saw an American white man for the first time. Two years earlier, in 1848, the United States had defeated Mexico in the Mexican War. Now part of the Apache territory was officially in the United States. The Apache were friendly to the Americans. They helped them find water holes and guided them through the mountains. In July 1852, Mangas Coloradas signed a treaty of peace between the Apache and the United States.

Around this time Geronimo began to rebuild his family. He married a Bedonkohe woman named Chee-hash-kish, and they had two children. Later he married another woman, Nana-tha-thtith, and they had one child. An Apache warrior had to be a good raider and hunter in order to provide for two families. Each year Geronimo led raiding parties down to Mexico. After one raid Mexican soldiers crossed the border and attacked his camp, or *rancheria*. They killed many women and children, including Nana-tha-thtith and her child. Still the raids continued, with Geronimo becoming more and more successful.

Relations between the Apache and the United States continued to be fairly peaceful through the 1850s. Travelers on the trail to southern California passed unharmed through Apache territory. In 1858 the Butterfield Stage Line was opened along the same route. Cochise, the great chief of the Chiricahua, protected travelers and provided wood for the stage station near Apache Pass.

In the summer of 1860, Mangas Coloradas visited a miners' camp in the heart of his territory. The miners treated the Indians badly, and they paid Mexican farmers—the Apache's enemy—to provide them with food. Mangas wanted to discuss the problems, but the miners tied the great chief to a tree and whipped him with a bullwhip. Mangas and Cochise went on the warpath. They destroyed the Mexicans' farms, attacked the miners' camps, and stole their livestock. Then they attacked a wagon train on the trail to California, killed 16 men, and stole 400 cattle and 900 sheep.

This incident passed, and there was still the possibility of peace. Then, in January 1861, Cochise met with a U.S. Army officer near Apache Pass. The officer, Lieutenant George Bascom, accused the Chiricahua chief of stealing a boy from a local ranch. Cochise truthfully said he knew nothing about the boy but that he would help Bascom find him. Bascom called Cochise a liar and threatened to hold him as a hostage until the boy was returned. Cochise pulled out his big knife, cut a hole in the army tent, and escaped into the night. Three Apache warriors were still held as hostages.

Cochise led his warriors, including Geronimo, and attacked the stage station at Apache Pass, capturing one man. Then they attacked a wagon train, killed eight Mexicans, and captured two Americans. Cochise offered to trade one of the Americans he held for the three warriors held by the Americans, but Bascom refused.

After two weeks of conflict, Cochise killed his hostages. The army hanged the three Apaches as well as three others who had nothing to do with the fighting. During the next two months, the warriors of Mangas and Cochise terrorized the countryside, killing more than 150 Americans and Mexicans.

Geronimo later said, "After this trouble all of the Indians agreed not to be friendly with the white men anymore . . . this treachery on the part of the soldiers had angered the Indians and revived memories of other wrongs, so that we never again trusted the United States troops."

In the summer of 1862, Cochise's warriors were defeated in a battle with U.S. solders at Apache Pass. By this time the Apache were armed with rifles they had taken from their victims, but they were no match for the soldiers' cannons. A large American military force moved through the pass and established Fort Bowie in the heart of Apache territory.

The following year Mangas Coloradas again tried to make peace with a group of miners. He was captured and turned over to U.S. soldiers, who tortured him with hot bayonets. When Mangas protested, they murdered him and said he was trying to escape. Geronimo believed that the murder of Mangas Coloradas was "perhaps the greatest wrong ever done to the Indians."

With the death of Mangas, Geronimo became the leader of the Bedonkohe, although he was probably never elected chief. In the fall of 1863, U.S. soldiers attacked Geronimo's *rancheria*, killed 16 Apache, stole their horses, and destroyed their property. Facing a bleak winter, Geronimo led his people to join the Warm Springs band in New Mexico. Later he and the Bedonkohe united with Cochise and the Chiricahua, who were still on the warpath.

During the 1860s, some American military leaders favored total extermination of the Apache—hunting and killing every Apache man, woman, and child. More humanitarian leaders wanted the Indians confined on reservations where they would be provided with food and supplies in return for giving up their land and their freedom. Many Apache were willing to try the reservations—if they included their homelands. In October 1870, 800 Warm Springs Apache settled on a reservation that included their traditional hunting ground.

In 1872, President Ulysses S. Grant sent General Oliver Howard to make peace with Cochise and other hostile Apache. Howard met with Cochise and his lieutenants, including Geronimo, and agreed to establish a reservation on the Chiricahua homeland in southeastern Arizona. In June of 1874, Cochise died on the reservation, and his oldest son, Taza, became chief of the Chiricahua Apache.

By the beginning of 1875, many Apache were settled on reservations that included their homelands. According to the agreements that formed the reservations, the land was theirs forever. This was all the Apache really wanted. They were willing to give the white man most of the territory, but they wanted to keep their traditional land for their children and their children's children.

Then in February 1875, the U.S. government began to move the Apache into smaller and smaller areas. Most of them were moved to the San Carlos Reservation, east of the current city of Phoenix, Arizona. There the land was low desert with hot summers, little vegetation, few animals, and diseases that the mountain Apache had never encountered. Some Apache groups were very different from others; some groups were even enemies. But at San Carlos, Apache from all over the West were thrown together in one place.

In June 1876, the Chiricahua were moved from the homeland they had been promised forever. When it was time to leave, Geronimo and Juh escaped. Juh, who was now the Nednai chief, led his people back to the Sierra Madre of Mexico. Geronimo led his followers to the Warm Springs Reservation in New Mexico.

Until his escape, Geronimo was not as well known as the other Apache leaders. Now he became infamous as a renegade. John Clum, the government agent at San Carlos, blamed Geronimo for every raid that occurred in the Chiricahua territory, even though Geronimo was in New Mexico. In April 1877, Clum arrested Geronimo on the Warm Springs Reservation and took him back to San Carlos in leg irons, along with 400 Warm Springs Apache. Geronimo remained in chains until Clum resigned in July.

The new agent ordered Geronimo released, but the Apache war leader continued to hate the San Carlos Reservation. Many of his fellow Apache were also unhappy because the young Chiricahua chief, Taza, had died mysteriously on a publicity trip to the East with John Clum. Naiche, Cochise's second son, succeeded his brother as chief. He was a brave warrior, but he was not trained to be a leader. Geronimo became the true leader of the Chiricahua Apache.

On April 4, 1878, Geronimo and Juh led a large group of Chiricahua in a mass escape from the San Carlos Reservation. They resumed their old life of raiding from the Sierra Madre and trading in the Mexican towns. Then, in August 1879, a group of

Geronimo

Warm Springs Apache under the leadership of Victorio fled from the Mescalero Reservation and began the most violent raiding in the history of the Southwest, inflaming fear and hatred of the Apache. A few months later, Geronimo and Juh returned to San Carlos and agreed to live in peace. But peace was not to last.

On August 29, 1881, American soldiers murdered an Apache religious leader north of the San Carlos Reservation. This sparked a battle in which 18 Indians and 8 soldiers were killed. A large military force was sent to San Carlos, and the Apache were afraid that the soldiers would turn against them. A month later Geronimo, Juh, and Naiche led another escape from the reservation into Mexico. They killed Americans along their way, including three soldiers.

In the Sierra Madre, Geronimo, Juh, and Naiche met up with around 20 survivors of Victorio's band. Mexican soldiers had killed or captured the rest of the band—almost 150 people, including Victorio. The renegades decided to raid the San Carlos Reservation and "free" the rest of the Warm Springs band, who were trying to live in peace. On April 19, 1882, Geronimo's raiding party forced several hundred Warm Springs Apache to leave the reservation. They included 30 warriors whom the renegades needed as reinforcements.

Once the fleeing Apache were across the Mexican border, Geronimo thought they were safe. However, two U.S. Army units followed them despite orders not to cross the border. Catching the Apache by surprise, the Americans stole most of their horses and killed 14 warriors before the Indians could retreat.

As the Apache continued on foot, the warriors stayed in the rear, watching for the Americans. The women and children walked directly into a Mexican infantry unit that slaughtered 78 Apache, including 67 women and children. Thirty-three women and children were taken prisoner. Geronimo led the survivors into the Sierra Madre, where they united with Juh's people. Despite their great losses, a large number of Apache were now gathered in one place.

On May 1, 1883, General George Crook—U.S. Army commander in Arizona—crossed the border on the trail of the renegades. Crook believed that the Indians must first be defeated by military strength before they would live peacefully on the reservations. However, he realized that the only way to fight Apache was with other Apache. He formed units of "friendly" Apache scouts who helped guide the Americans into the wild Apache territory.

With 50 soldiers and 200 Apache scouts, Crook climbed higher and higher into the Sierra Madre until he found Geronimo's camp.

Geronimo was not there, having taken some warriors to the town of Casas Grandes, 120 miles away. One night he said, "Men, our people we left at base camp are in the hands of U.S. soldiers. What shall we do?" The warriors believed in Geronimo's Power and decided to go back. When they arrived at their base camp, Geronimo realized that he was beaten. The American were in his stronghold; the Mexicans were allowing the Americans to cross the border; and his own people—the Apache scouts—were working against him. He and most of the other leaders agreed to surrender. Only Juh continued to fight, but he had lost most of his warriors.

On May 24, Crook left the mountains with over 300 Apache. Geronimo promised to follow as soon as he gathered his people. Nine months later, in February 1884, Geronimo finally arrived at the U.S. border. He had not only gathered his people, but he had also stolen 350 Mexican cattle along the way. Geronimo considered this his right. He had made peace with the Americans, not with the Mexicans. But Crook took the cattle away when Geronimo reached the San Carlos Reservation. Thus once again Geronimo began his life on the reservation in anger.

After Geronimo arrived, the Chiricahua and Warm Springs Apache were moved to their own section of the reservation. The new land was a mountain area with animals to hunt, water to drink, and trees to use for houses. It would have been a good home if the Apache had been allowed to raise cattle. This was Geronimo's plan, and the local military officers agreed with him. However, the U.S. government wanted all the Indians to become farmers, regardless of their experience or the type of land on their reservation. So the Apache tried to become farmers.

By the spring of 1885, the Apache were beginning to adapt to the new way of life. Even Geronimo had a small farm. But many of the warriors were restless and angry. They felt that the government was interfering with their traditional way of life. The biggest conflict was over a mild alcoholic beverage called *tizwin*, which was forbidden on the reservation. After a mass protest by Indian leaders, Geronimo was afraid he would be thrown in prison. On May 17, he convinced over 140 Apache to leave the reservation.

Once again Geronimo led his people to the Sierra Madre where they met the remaining Nednai. Juh was dead now, and Geronimo was the leader of all the renegade bands. That summer U.S. troops followed the Apache into Mexico and captured many women and children, including two of Geronimo's wives and all his children. Geronimo led a daring raid back to San Carlos, where he recovered his wife She-gha and their three-year-old daughter.

During the fall of 1885, Geronimo continued to raid Mexican towns from his stronghold in the Sierra Madre. But in January 1886, American troops captured Geronimo's empty *rancheria*. Once again, the Americans had demonstrated that they could penetrate his mountain fortress. Geronimo offered to meet with General Crook to discuss peace.

Geronimo with three of the warriors who fought with him until the end (l. to r.): Yahnozha, Chappo (Geronimo's son), and Fun. This photograph was taken during the second peace conference with General Crook in March 1886.
(Fort Sill Museum. Photograph by Camillus S. Fly)

On March 25, 1886, General Crook and the Chiricahua leaders held a conference in northern Mexican, about 10 miles south of the Arizona border. Geronimo acted as the Indian spokesman. He said that he was a good man, Crook was a good man, and all the trouble was stirred up by dishonest agents and interpreters who did not repeat his words correctly. He believed that there had been a plot against him, and the newspapers were calling for his death. That was why he had left. Now he was willing to go back to the reservation, forget the past, and live in peace.

Crook said Geronimo was a liar and that he had two choices: He could either surrender unconditionally, or Crook would pursue him until the last warrior was dead. After further negotiations, Crook made a better offer: The warriors would be imprisoned for two years in the East, and they could have their families with them. On March 27, Geronimo, Naiche, and another leader named Chihuahua surrendered on Crook's terms.

Crook left the next morning, and the Indians were supposed to follow with an officer and a group of Apache scouts. However, an American trader sold the Indians liquor, and they got drunk for two days. Even worse, the trader told Geronimo that he would be hanged as soon as he crossed the border. When the Apache left on the morning of March 29, Geronimo and Naiche slipped away with 18 warriors and 20 women and children. Chihuahua and his people continued on to prison.

At his own request, General Crook was relieved of his command. He was replaced by General Nelson A. Miles. Unlike Crook, who used small troops of tough soldiers and Apache scouts, Miles tried to pursue Geronimo with 5,000 men. In five months Miles and his army failed to kill or capture a single Apache. Four thousand Mexican soldiers were equally unsuccessful. Geronimo's warriors raided on both sides of the border, stealing supplies and leaving a trail of dead bodies.

Frustrated in his attempts to capture Geronimo, Miles decided to move all the Chiricahua and Warm Springs Apache from the San Carlos Reservation to Fort Marion in St. Augustine, Florida. Although these were the "good Indians" who had stayed on the reservation peacefully, they were treated like prisoners of war.

In August 1886, Miles sent Lieutenant Charles Gatewood with two Indian guides to make contact with Geronimo. Gatewood found the renegade warrior and told him that there was no longer a reservation for his people—that they were all in Florida. He promised that the warriors could be with their families. Geronimo wanted to keep fighting, but some of his warriors were tired of battle. Geronimo said that he would meet with General Miles.

On September 3, General Miles met Geronimo and Naiche in Skeleton Canyon, 10 miles north of the Mexican border. Miles repeated the promise that the warriors would be reunited with their families in Florida. After the reunion they would be given a separate reservation with houses and horses and all that they needed to live a good life. The past would be wiped out. They would live in peace. On September 4, 1886, Geronimo and Naiche officially surrendered to General Miles and the United States. The Indian Wars were over.

The Apache prisoners of war sitting beside the Southern Pacific Railroad in Texas, on their way to prison camps in Florida. Naiche, hereditary chief of the Chiricahua Apache, sits in the center; Geronimo and his son, Chappo, sit to Naiche's left wearing matching shirts. September 10, 1886.
(Fort Sill Museum. Photograph by A. J. McDonald)

Despite Miles's promises, Geronimo and his warriors were held as prisoners of war—without their families—at Fort Pickens off the coast of Pensacola, Florida. Ironically, the living conditions of the renegade warriors were better than the conditions in which the "good Indians" lived. At Fort Marion, hundreds of Apache were crowded into a small space. They were not given enough food, and many died of malaria or tuberculosis.

In 1887 all the Chiricahua and Warm Springs Apache, including Geronimo's warriors, were moved to Mount Vernon Barracks in Alabama. Five years later they were moved to Fort Sill, Oklahoma. Both of these were military bases where the Indians were allowed to live as families but were still guarded and treated like prisoners of war. Although conditions were better, they continued to suffer from malaria and tuberculosis. In the first three and a half years of captivity, 89 Apache died in the camps and 30 children died at the Carlisle Indian School—a boarding school in Pennsylvania where Indian children were sent to be "civilized."

During his final months as a free Apache raider, Geronimo had been the most feared and hated Indian in America; as a prisoner of war, he became a celebrity. Tourists paid him for his pictures, autographs, and bows and arrows. He was allowed to appear at expositions and fairs, including the 1904 Louisiana Purchase Exposition in St. Louis. In 1905 Geronimo was invited to ride in President Theodore Roosevelt's inaugural parade. Later he met the president and made a passionate plea for his people:

"Great Father, other Indians have homes where they can live and be happy. I and my people have no homes. The place where we are kept is bad for us . . . We are sick there and we die . . . Let me die in my own country, an old man who has been punished enough and is free."

President Roosevelt was sympathetic, but he told Geronimo that the white people of Arizona would stir up too much trouble if the Apache returned.

On February 17, 1909, Geronimo died at Fort Sill, Oklahoma, after 23 years as a prisoner of war. Three years later, on August 24, 1912, the U.S. Congress passed a law releasing the Apache as prisoners. The following year 183 Chiricahua and Warm Springs Apache moved to the reservation of the Mescalero Apache in New Mexico. Seventy-eight decided to stay on small farms in Oklahoma. Thus, out of several thousand Southern Apache who had roamed the Southwest less than 100 years earlier, only 261 remained.

After Geronimo surrendered, an American citizen sued the Apache and the United States for losses caused by Geronimo's raiders. The federal judge presiding over the case described

Geronimo

Geronimo wearing ceremonial Apache headdress.
Note how different it is from the headdress worn
by Sitting Bull on p. 1.
(Fort Sill Museum)

Geronimo's final campaign as follows: "There is not, probably, in the history of traditions or myths of the human race another instance of such prolonged resistance against such tremendous odds."

At the time of his surrender Geronimo was almost 60 years old. What kind of man could fight so hard for so long? Who was Geronimo? General Miles, who negotiated the surrender, described him as "one of the brightest, most resolute, determined looking men that I have ever encountered . . . Every movement indicated power, energy and determination. In everything he did, he had a purpose."

The white settlers of Arizona had a different opinion. To them Geronimo was a killer and raider who left nothing but death and destruction in his path. The newspapers demanded his capture and execution. Men like Wyatt Earp joined posses to bring him to justice. Even Grover Cleveland, then president of the United States, wanted to see him hanged.

The Apache also had conflicting opinions about Geronimo. Some who wanted to live peacefully on the reservations considered him a troublemaker who caused innocent people to be punished for his actions. But others looked to him as a leader who resisted the white man with the proud spirit of an Apache warrior. The Apache will only follow a leader they respect. Geronimo was never officially a chief, but chiefs and warriors followed him.

A century later, Geronimo seems more like a patriot than a criminal. Yes, he killed and stole, but those he was fighting—first the Mexicans, then the Americans—killed his people and stole his land. Perhaps he lied, but from his point of view he always kept his word. And there is no question that the white man lied to him more than he ever lied to the white man.

Ironically, Geronimo had great respect for Americans. He called them "a great people," and he truly wanted to live with them in peace. Like most Indian leaders, he was more than willing to share his land with the white-skinned newcomers. But that wasn't enough for the people of America. They wanted everything—and they got it through violence and trickery. Everything, that is, except the spirit of people like Geronimo.

Chronology

▬▬▬▬▬▬

c. 1829	Goyahkla (Geronimo) is born near the headwaters of the Gila River in southeastern Arizona
c. 1850	His wife, children, and mother are killed by Mexican soldiers
January 1861	Lieutenant Bascom tries to take Cochise hostage; this marks the end of good relations between the Apache and the United States
January 18, 1863	Mangas Coloradas is murdered by U.S. soldiers
June 1876	Chiricahua Apache are moved to San Carlos Reservation; Geronimo and Juh escape
April 21, 1877	Geronimo is arrested on the Warm Springs Reservation
April 4, 1878	Geronimo and Juh lead the Chiricahua off the San Carlos Reservation
September 30, 1881	Geronimo, Juh, and Naiche lead a second escape from San Carlos
May 1883	General Crook occupies Geronimo's camp in the Sierra Madre; Geronimo agrees to surrender
May 17, 1885	Geronimo leads a third escape from San Carlos
March 27–29, 1886	Surrenders to General Crook for a second time; escapes on the way to the United States
September 4, 1886	Surrenders to General Miles
February 17, 1909	Geronimo dies at Fort Sill, Oklahoma
August 24, 1912	Chiricahua and Warm Springs Apache are released as prisoners of war

Further Reading

Young Adult Books

Shorto, Russell. *Geronimo and the Struggle for Apache Freedom*. Englewood Cliffs, NJ: Silver Burdett Press, 1989. The most recent biography for young readers; includes illustrations and bibliography; 129 pp.

Syme, Ronald. *Geronimo the Fighting Apache*. New York: William Morrow & Company, 1975. A short biography written in a storytelling style; some inaccuracies but good examination of Geronimo's character; 96 pp.

Wilson, Charles Morrow. *Geronimo*. Minneapolis: Dillon Press, 1973. A short biography written in a straightforward, factual style; 76 pp.

Adult Books

Adams, Alexander B. *Geronimo*. New York: G. P. Putnam's Sons, 1971. A well-written biography that is clear enough for some younger readers.

Debo, Angie. *Geronimo: The Man, His Time, His Place*. Norman: University of Oklahoma Press, 1976. The most complete biography; too difficult for young readers, but excellent for librarians or parents who want the complete story.

Geronimo. *Geronimo's Story of His Life*, taken down and edited by S. M. Barrett. New York: Duffield & Company, 1906. A fascinating book that provides Geronimo's side of the story; there are inaccuracies in dates and other facts due to Geronimo's advanced age and Barrett's poor understanding of Apache customs.

Belle Starr:
A Lady Among Outlaws

Belle Starr, posing with her pistols in
Fort Smith, Arkansas, 1887.
(Western History Collections, University of
Oklahoma Library; Payne Collection)

*B*elle Starr—the Bandit Queen! The Female Jesse James! The
Queen of the Outlaws! She rode with Confederate guerrillas
during the Civil War and killed four men by the time she was 18.
She married Cole Younger—the famous partner of Jesse James—

and when Cole left her with a child, she took her anger out on the world. She was a beautiful woman who wrapped men around her fingers and led the most dangerous outlaw gang in the Indian Territory. As a criminal, she dressed in men's clothing and killed anyone who got in her way. As a lady, she dressed in fine gowns and mingled with high society.

This is the legend of Belle Starr. It's quite a story, and it has entertained readers and moviegoers for almost a century. Unfortunately, not a single word of it is true. The legend began during Belle's lifetime, but the real confusion started with a small paperback that appeared shortly after Belle's death in 1889. It was entitled *Bella Starr, the Bandit Queen, or The Female Jesse James.* Burton Rascoe, a later biographer of Starr, wrote of the 1889 book: "This narrative does not have a single essential fact correct: her name and date of birth are both wrong . . . "

Most other biographers—including Rascoe—also had problems with the facts of Belle's life. Finally, in 1982, western historian Glenn Shirley wrote a biography called *Belle Starr and Her Times* that separated the facts from the legends. Shirley consulted court records, letters, local newspapers, and personal interviews to find the truth about Belle Starr. It's still quite a story.

———

Belle Starr was born on February 5, 1848, on a large farm in southwestern Missouri. Her given name was Myra Maybelle Shirley. In the early 1850s, her father, John Shirley, sold the farm and built a successful hotel and blacksmith shop in the growing town of Carthage, Missouri. Myra attended the Carthage Female Academy where she studied classical subjects and learned to play the piano. A schoolmate later remembered her as intelligent but quick to fight. When she wasn't in school, Myra often went riding with her older brother, Bud, who taught her to shoot a rifle and a pistol.

Myra's pleasant childhood ended with the beginning of the Civil War in 1861. Although Missouri remained officially in the Union, many Missourians fought with the Confederacy as unofficial troops called guerrillas. Bud Shirley joined a group of Confederate guerrillas and became one of the most wanted rebels in southwest Missouri. According to legend, Myra rode swiftly through the countryside to warn her brother that Union soldiers were about to capture him. There is no evidence for this, but it is quite possible. According to another legend, Myra herself rode with a group of Confederate guerrillas under the famous William Quantrill. This is nonsense.

In June 1864, Bud Shirley was killed by Union troops. Myra and her mother claimed the body. An eyewitness reported that Myra wore two big revolvers on her waist and swore revenge for Bud's death. That summer John Shirley packed his family and belongings into two Conestoga wagons and headed for Texas. His prosperous business had been ruined by theft and destruction during the war.

The Shirleys settled on a farm in Scyene, Texas, just east of Dallas. According to legend, the family was visited during the summer of 1866 by Jesse James and the Younger brothers, who were in Texas to get rid of money from a bank robbery. It was supposedly during this visit that Cole Younger seduced or secretly married Myra and fathered her child. It is true that the Shirleys knew Cole Younger from Missouri and that he visited them in Texas. However, the visit occurred in 1864 and there was never a romance between Cole Younger and Myra Shirley.

In fact, Myra married another man from Missouri who had ridden with the James and Younger brothers during the Civil War. His name was James C. Reed, and Myra had known him in Carthage. They were married in Collin County, Texas, on November 1, 1866. Myra was 18; Jim was 20. Shortly after the wedding the newlyweds returned to Missouri, where they lived on Jim's family farm. In September 1868, Myra gave birth to a daughter, Rosie Lee Reed. Myra called her "Pearl."

While Myra and Pearl stayed home in Missouri, Jim Reed joined an Arkansas gang that stole livestock and smuggled whiskey into Indian Territory. After a violent feud with another gang, Reed was wanted for murder. He picked up Myra and Pearl and went to Los Angeles, California. There, on February 22, 1871, Myra gave birth to a son named James Edward (Eddie) Reed. The next month federal authorities accused Jim Reed of passing counterfeit money. During the investigation they discovered the Arkansas murder charge. Reed fled to Texas, with Myra and the two children following.

John Shirley gave the Reeds a small farm in Bosque County, Texas. Jim Reed wasn't much of a farmer, however, so he and his brother Sol began stealing cattle and horses. In February 1873, they killed a man while stealing his livestock. A few months later they killed one of their partners who was talking too much. The governor of Texas offered rewards for both Reed brothers. Jim and Myra left the children with Myra's parents and escaped to the Indian Territory.

On November 19, 1873, Jim Reed and two other men robbed a wealthy Creek Indian farmer named Watt Grayson. Grayson, who was 65 years old, was hanged twice before he finally revealed the location of his treasure—more than $30,000 in gold. According to legend, Myra was also involved in the robbery, dressed as a man. There is no evidence of this. Myra later admitted that she saw her husband and his partners dividing up the gold. Her only "crime" at this point in her life was being the wife of an outlaw.

After the robbery Jim and Myra returned to Texas. Then Jim Reed abandoned his family and went to San Antonio with an 18-year-old woman named Rosa McCommas. On April 7, 1874, Reed and two partners robbed the stagecoach between San Antonio and Austin, escaping with $3,000 and one bag of U.S. mail. Reed was now one of the most wanted men in Texas. After a series of narrow escapes, Jim Reed was killed by a special deputy on August 6, 1874.

Although Myra was hurt by Reed's relationship with Rosa McCommas, she never lost her love for him. In August 1876, she wrote a letter to Reed's family in which she referred to "the dear one that's gone" and complained that his brother Sol did not avenge Jim's death. In the same letter, Myra bragged about her children. "[Eddie] is a fine, manly looking boy . . . and is said to resemble Jimmie very much . . . I don't think there is a more intelligent boy living . . . [Rosie] has the reputation of being the prettiest little girl in Dallas. She had been playing on the stage here in the Dallas theatre and gained a world-wide reputation for her prize performance."

Myra apparently sold her farm shortly after writing this letter. There is some evidence that she lived in Kansas during the next few years with Bruce Younger, a noted horse thief and a relative of the more famous Cole Younger. While living with Bruce, she may have called her daughter "Pearl Younger," which led to the rumor that the girl was Cole Younger's daughter.

On June 5, 1880, Myra married Sam Starr, the son of the famous Cherokee outlaw Tom Starr. The elder Starr had been a friend of Jim Reed and was also a good friend of the Younger family. Sam was 23 years old, tall and very handsome. Myra was 32 but claimed to be 27. By this time she was using the name "Belle Reed." Thus, with her marriage to Sam Starr she became "Belle Starr."

Belle Starr

Sam, Belle, and Pearl settled along the Canadian River in the Cherokee Nation. Eddie lived with Jim Reed's mother in Missouri. The Starr ranch was near a big bend in the river called Youngers' Bend. According to legend, Belle named it after her long-lost love, Cole Younger. In fact, Tom Starr named it in honor of the Youngers long before Belle ever saw it.

Sometime in 1881 Jesse James visited Belle, whom he knew through Jim Reed and the Youngers. Jesse was on the run, and Belle was not eager to hide him. But she put him up for several weeks and introduced him to her husband as Mr. Williams. This visit from the famous outlaw has caused many biographers to imagine Belle's ranch as an outlaw hotel where the worst desperadoes came and went as honored guests. According to some stories, Belle led her outlaw pals on daring crime sprees throughout the Indian Territory. It is true that Belle knew some pretty tough characters, but there is no evidence that she ever led an outlaw gang.

On April 20, 1882, Belle Starr finally committed a crime. Apparently, she and Sam stole two horses belonging to two different neighbors. The Starrs led the horses into the corral of another neighbor named John West and later sold them with their own herd. On July 31, Belle and Sam were arrested by U.S. Deputy Marshal L. W. Marks. According to Marks's wife, Belle "fought like a tiger and threatened to kill the officers." She had two derringer pistols in the top of her dress and a six-shooter under her skirt. On the way back to court—a journey of many days—Belle escaped once and was so difficult that she finally had to be chained.

On October 9, a hearing was held in Fort Smith, Arkansas. The chief witness against the Starrs was John West, the man whose pen they had used to corral the horses. This was the beginning of a feud between Sam Starr and the West family that ultimately led to disaster. On February 15–19, 1883, Belle and Sam were tried before Judge Isaac Parker, the famous "Hanging Judge" of the U.S. District Court.

Until her trial, Belle Starr was unknown outside of her family and friends. Now she became famous—or infamous—in the local newspapers. The *Fort Smith New Era* reported, "The very idea of a woman being charged with an offense of this kind and that she was the leader of a band of horse thieves and wielding a power over them as their queen and guiding spirit, was sufficient to fill the courtroom with spectators." This was the birth of Belle Starr the Bandit Queen.

After one hour of deliberation, the jury found Belle and Sam guilty. On March 8, Judge Parker sentenced them each to one year in the House of Correction at Detroit, Michigan. They were released in December 1883, after nine months in prison, with three months off for good behavior. Belle picked up Pearl along the way and the three of them returned to Youngers' Bend. In 1884 Eddie Reed also came to live with them. For the first time in eight years, Belle and her two children were together.

Belle Starr, on her beloved black mare, Venus, *in Fort Smith, Arkansas, May 23, 1886. Belle was in town to put up bond in the farm robbery case.*
(Archives & Manuscripts Division of the Oklahoma Historical Society. Photograph by Rhoeder's Gallery)

Belle Starr

After her release from prison, Belle began to act the part of the Bandit Queen. Perched on a fancy sidesaddle, she rode through the streets of Fort Smith on Venus, her big black mare. She wore a black velvet riding outfit, a turned-up sombrero with a bright feather, and expensive leather boots that showed off her dainty feet. Strapped to her waist was a Colt .45 revolver, which she called "my baby." Although there are wild stories about her behavior, most people from Fort Smith later remembered her as being very dignified and ladylike.

On one trip to town, Belle bought a piano for $50 and then paid a wagon driver another $50 to cart the heavy instrument to Youngers' Bend. The story shows two sides of Belle's character. On the one hand, she was a cultured woman who brought a piano into the rough wilderness of the Indian Territory. On the other hand, she had $100 in cash—a fair amount of money in those days—to spend on a luxury item. Where did she get it?

In December 1884, an outlaw named John Middleton asked Belle and Sam for help in hiding from the law. The Starrs hid Middleton until the following May, when Belle and Pearl smuggled him away from the ranch in a wagon. Middleton bought an old one-eyed horse from an acquaintance of Belle; apparently neither Belle nor Middleton knew that the horse was stolen. The outlaw borrowed a saddle from Pearl and a Colt .45 from Belle and headed for Arkansas. Along the way he drowned trying to cross a river. The horse was found nearby, with Pearl's saddle and Belle's Colt .45. It looked as if Belle had stolen the horse.

The next month Sam Starr was in more serious trouble. On June 15, 1885, the U.S. mail was robbed in the Cherokee Nation, and a warrant for Sam was issued. However, the identification was vague and the warrant was never served. Then on October 30, three men burglarized a store and U.S. post office in the Choctaw Nation. One of them was positively identified as Sam Starr. The two others were later arrested but Sam stayed on the run.

In January 1886, a warrant was issued for Belle in the theft of the one-eyed horse. Belle surrendered to a U.S. marshal and pleaded not guilty before Judge Parker. After posting bond, she was released. Three weeks later, on February 27, three men robbed a farm in the Choctaw Nation. Most of the people on the farm could not identify the robbers. However, a young woman not only identified one of the robbers, but claimed "he" was Belle Starr dressed in man's clothing. Belle was accused of being the gang leader of the farm robbery and arrested in mid-May. Once again she posted bond and was released.

At the end of June, there was a hearing into the robbery. The young woman stuck to her story, but the other witnesses made it clear that each of the three robbers was too big to be a woman, particularly a woman who was built like Belle. Although Belle's face was somewhat masculine in her later years, her body was quite feminine. The case was dismissed.

In September, Belle was found not guilty on the charge of stealing the one-eyed horse. The man who sold the horse to John Middleton—and who should have been accused of the crime—testified that he saw a stranger sell it to the outlaw. He also paid Belle's court costs. Belle was now completely free of all legal accusations, but Sam Starr was still on the run—and in trouble.

While Belle was in Fort Smith for the trial, Sam was shot and wounded by a sheriff's posse. Sam escaped, but Belle's black mare, Venus, was killed in the shootout. The man who fired the shots was Frank West, John West's brother. When Belle returned, she convinced Sam to turn himself in to the court in Fort Smith. In October, Sam posted bond and was released until his trial.

On December 17, Sam and Belle went to a Christmas party on the other side of the Canadian River. Belle played the organ, accompanied by a fiddler and the party-goers danced to the music. Around the end of the first dance, Frank West arrived and warmed his hands at a big fire at the bottom of the hill. Someone told Sam, and he quietly slipped away, leaving Belle and the dancers. At the bottom of the hill, Sam drew his revolver and shot West. West drew his revolver and shot Sam. They both fell before the fire and died.

After Sam's death, Belle had no legal right to live at Youngers' Bend. According to Cherokee law, the land could be held only by a Cherokee. Belle solved the problem by inviting a handsome young Indian named Bill July to live with her as man and wife. Bill was 24; Belle was 39. Although they had no marriage certificate, their marriage was legal according to Cherokee custom and U.S. common law.

Around the time that Bill July moved into Youngers' Bend, Belle decided to go straight. She publicly announced that she would no longer allow outlaws to stay on her land. In July 1887, she received a letter from the U.S. Indian agent congratulating her on her new, respectable attitude. The next month, when Bill July was arrested for stealing a horse, Belle refused to help him.

Ironically, it was Belle's attempt at respectability that led to her death. Toward the end of 1888, she agreed to rent some farmland to a neighbor named Edgar Watson. However, she backed out on the deal when she discovered that Watson was wanted for murder in Florida. She and Watson argued, and Belle hinted that she knew about the murder charge.

On February 2, 1889, Belle accompanied Bill July partway to Fort Smith, where he was going for his trial. The following day she rode back toward Youngers' Bend, stopping at a neighbor's house along the way. There were many people gathered, including Edgar Watson, who disappeared shortly after Belle arrived. Around 4:30 in the afternoon, Belle left for home, riding toward the Canadian River. She was ambushed and shot twice with a shotgun. The first blast was from the back; the second was in the face.

When Belle's horse returned to Youngers' Bend without its rider, Pearl crossed the river and found her mother lying in the mud. Belle was still alive, but she died without saying a word. The next morning Eddie Reed followed the murderer's tracks. They disappeared near Edgar Watson's place. Watson wore the same size boot as the one that made the tracks. He had a shotgun like the one that killed Belle. It added up.

One of the log cabins on Belle Starr's homestead at Youngers' Bend.
(Archives & Manuscript Division of the Oklahoma Historical Society;
Rucker Collection)

Belle was buried beside her cabin at Youngers' Bend, dressed in her black velvet riding outfit and holding her favorite pistol in her hand. The neighbors, including Edgar Watson, gathered around the grave. When the funeral was over, Bill July forced Watson into Fort Smith at the end of a rifle. Watson was released after a hearing, because the evidence was considered circumstantial. Some biographers have tried to pin Belle's murder on a wide variety of characters, including Eddie Reed, Bill July, Tom Starr, and John Reed's brother. But the evidence points to Watson. He later returned to Florida, where he was accused of several more murders and killed by a group of neighbors.

Belle Starr was a well-educated young lady who became the most famous female outlaw in the history of the Wild West. How did it happen? Belle knew many dangerous outlaws, including Cole Younger and Jesse James. She was married to three, maybe four, men who rode on the wrong side of the law. And she occasionally allowed her outlaw friends to hide at the Starr ranch. But there is no evidence that Belle Starr ever did anything more illegal than steal two horses.

If Belle were only a horse thief, she would still have attracted attention simply because she was a woman. However, the fact that Belle was an educated white woman married to Sam Starr—an Indian who could not read or write—was enough to make many people believe that she was a gang leader, the brains of the operation. It is possible that Belle *was* the leader of the Starr gang. But there are two strong arguments against it. First, there is no evidence. Second, Sam Starr was the son of Tom Starr, who was famous as an outlaw in the Indian Territory long before Belle arrived. Sam Starr was raised on crime. It seems unlikely that he would let Belle run the operation.

Still, Belle was an unusual, strong-willed woman who managed to get into more than her share of trouble. Like most men and women of her time and place, she was a product of the Civil War. Outlaws like Jesse James, Cole Younger, and Jim Reed were educated young men from good families who turned to crime after losing the war. Belle—who also supported the losing side—married one of these men, and it seems that there was no turning back.

Belle Starr

In 1910 Frederick Barde wrote, "There are still persons living in old Indian Territory who feel that she was more sinned against than sinning . . . the victim of surroundings from which she could not escape."

A few months before she died, Belle put it like this: "I regard myself as a woman who has seen much of life."

Chronology

February 5, 1848	Myra Maybelle Shirley (Belle Starr) is born in Jasper County, Missouri
November 1, 1866	Marries James C. (Jim) Reed in Collin County, Texas
September 1868	Rosie Lee (Pearl) Reed is born
February 22, 1871	James Edward (Eddie) Reed is born
August 6, 1874	Jim Reed is killed by special deputy
June 5, 1880	Belle marries Sam Starr in the Cherokee Nation
April 20, 1882	Belle and Sam steal two horses
February 19, 1883	Bell and Sam are found guilty of horse theft
April 1885	Belle and Pearl help John Middleton to escape
February 27, 1886	A farm is robbed in the Choctaw Nation; Belle is accused of being the gang leader
June 29, 1886	Belle is discharged after a hearing into the farm robbery
September 30, 1886	Is found not guilty of stealing a one-eyed horse for John Middleton
December 17, 1886	Sam Starr is killed at a Christmas party
February 3, 1889	Belle Starr is ambushed and murdered near Youngers' Bend

Further Reading

Young Adult Books

There are apparently no young adult biographies of Belle Starr. There are short sections on Belle in a few books for younger children, but they are not very accurate.

Adult Books

Shirley, Glenn. *Belle Starr and Her Times: The Literature, the Facts, and the Legends.* Norman: University of Oklahoma Press, 1982. This is the only accurate biography of Belle Starr's life; however, the style is difficult, even for adults.

Judge Roy Bean:
Law West of the Pecos

Judge Roy Bean.
(Western History Collections, University of
Oklahoma Library; Rose Collection.
Photograph by Leach & Co., Llano, Texas)

*T*he dead man lay stretched out on the pool table, right in the middle of the saloon/courtroom. The grizzled old judge walked around the body as if he were measuring it for size. No one knew the dead man's name, so the judge searched his pockets for identification. He found out the man's name was O'Brien. He also found $40 and a six-shooter.

The judge stepped back and thumbed his old dusty lawbook, the *Revised Statutes of Texas* for 1879. After thinking about the situation for a while, he turned to the coroner's jury and the other men hanging around the saloon.

"Gentlemen," he said, "that man fell from the bridge and that's all there is about it. But there is one thing that is not so plain, and that is what was he doing with that gun? Of course he's dead and can't explain, but that ain't the fault of the law; it's his own misfortune. Justice is justice, and law is law, and as he can't offer no satifactory explanation of the matter I shall be obliged to fine him forty dollars for carrying a concealed weapon."

Welcome to the court of Judge Roy Bean, the Law West of the Pecos. Not to mention the coroner and the best saloon-keeper. For 20 years, Roy Bean was a legend throughout the Southwest. Texas Rangers, Mexican shepherds, and New York tourists came to his combination courtroom and saloon for justice, whiskey, and entertainment. The justice and whiskey were a little on the shady side, but the entertainment was first rate.

Roy Bean was born around 1825 in Mason County, Kentucky. His parents, Francis and Anna Bean, were sharecroppers who were apparently the "poor relations" of the Bean family. Roy had two older brothers, Joshua and Sam, who both played an important part in his life.

Like most frontier children, Roy probably spent a few months in school. He was able to read and write, although his writing was slow and hesitant. Around the age of 16, Roy traveled down the Mississippi River to New Orleans, with a boat taking slaves to market. He got into some sort of trouble and returned to Kentucky fairly quickly. It was the first of many quick escapes for the future judge.

In 1848, Roy joined his brother Sam in a trip to the Southwest. They bought a wagon, mules, and trading goods in Independence, Missouri, and set off across the Great American Desert for Santa Fe, New Mexico. Today we call this region the Great Plains, but to early pioneers like Roy and Sam Bean, it seemed like a treeless desert with no settlements, very little water, and plenty of hostile Indians.

In Santa Fe, the Bean brothers decided to continue on to Chihuahua, Mexico, where American goods brought a higher price. There they set up a small trading post, and Roy quickly adapted to Mexican ways. He liked the beautiful dark-eyed senoritas, the hot food, and the easy way of life. Unfortunately, the fun in Chihuahua didn't last. According to one story, Roy shot and killed a tough Mexican who was attacking him. Bean considered it self-defense, but the Mexican people considered it murder, so they drove all the American traders out of Chihuahua. Sam stayed in Mexico and married a woman he had met in Chihuahua. Roy continued north to San Diego.

When Bean arrived in San Diego, his oldest brother Joshua was *alcalde*, a Spanish term for a top official. In 1850, when California became a state, Joshua Bean became the first mayor of San Diego and the major general of the state militia. As the brother of such an important man, Roy enjoyed a high position in local society. The following year, when Joshua left to set up his headquarters near Los Angeles, Roy stayed behind.

Shortly after his brother's departure, Bean engaged in a duel on horseback with a man named Collins. Although dueling was against the law, a crowd of eager spectators watched Bean shoot Collins in the leg and kill his horse. Afterward the sheriff arrested both men, and Bean spent two months in the San Diego jail. In April 1852, he escaped and headed north to join Joshua. According to Bean, he dug his way out of the jail using tools supplied by his many female admirers.

In the town of San Gabriel, a few miles north of Los Angeles, General Joshua Bean had his headquarters in the old Spanish mission. He also owned a thriving establishment called the Headquarters Saloon. Roy worked for Joshua as a bartender, and he once again enjoyed the good life. In November 1852, Joshua Bean was murdered on his way home from the saloon. Many people believed his death was ordered by the famous bandit leader, Joaquin Murrieta, because of a conflict over a beautiful woman.

After Joshua's death, Roy took over the Headquarters Saloon. He was in his mid-twenties now, and though he grieved for his older brother, he enjoyed the life of a prosperous saloon-keeper. He dressed in elegant Mexican clothing and presided over his business with a quick mind and a good sense of humor. Once again, however, the fun didn't last.

According to Bean, a Mexican officer wanted to marry a certain senorita, but the senorita didn't want to marry the officer. Bean saved the young lady, and the officer challenged him to a duel in which Bean killed the officer. The officer's friends captured Bean and hung him from a tree. Fortunately, the rope stretched just enough to let Bean's toes touch the ground, keeping him alive until the senorita came to rescue him. In his later years, Bean still had a rope burn across his neck, and his neck was so stiff that he could not turn his head from side to side.

Around 1858 Bean joined his brother Sam in Mesilla, New Mexico. Sam owned a combination store and saloon as well as a freighting business. Roy was completely broke, so Sam took him into the business. The brothers were successful until the outbreak of the Civil War. Most people in New Mexico supported the Union, but the citizens of Mesilla and Tucson, including Roy and Sam Bean, voted to support the Confederacy. As Kentuckians, the Beans considered themselves Southerners.

In the summer of 1861, an army under Confederate General John R. Baylor marched in from Texas and occupied Mesilla. Although there is no record of his military service, Roy Bean claimed that he served under Baylor as a spy and scout. He also rode with a group of Confederate supporters called the Free Rovers. Many local citizens called them the "Forty Thieves" for their habit of stealing valuable goods in the name of the Confederacy.

In 1862 the Union army drove the Confederates out of New Mexico and back into Texas. Roy Bean settled in San Antonio. At the time, Union ships were blockading the Gulf of Mexico, preventing supplies from reaching the Confederate soldiers. Bean became a blockade runner, transporting Southern cotton to the Mexican port of Matamoros, where British cargo ships were waiting. He then returned to Texas with goods that were needed by the Southerners. As a Confederate sympathizer, Bean felt that he was doing his patriotic duty. As a businessman, he didn't mind getting rich.

By the end of the war, Bean had a successful freight business, with many horses, mules, and wagons. He was a tough businessman who didn't worry much about honesty, and he made many enemies in San Antonio. In 1866 he faced three different lawsuits. Although he was probably guilty in all three, he managed to win them through shrewd bluffing and use of the legal process.

One case involved Bean's house on the outskirts of San Antonio. The problem was that Bean didn't own it, and the man who *did* own it didn't know that Bean was living there. When the owner sold the property to another man, they were both surprised to discover that Roy Bean was living in the house and refused to move. After months of legal maneuvering, Bean finally agreed to move on the following condition: The new owner had to pay his expenses to resettle in an area of town that would be called Beanville. As a side deal, Bean sold the other man 40 mules and horses, six wagons, and a two-horse buggy for $3,000.

In the fall of 1866, Roy Bean moved to Beanville. He was the richest and most important citizen of a poor rundown neighborhood. This suited Bean fine. It was easier to be a big fish in a small pond, especially a small pond that was named after the fish.

Shortly after his arrival in Beanville, on October 28, 1866, Roy Bean married 18-year-old Virginia Chavez. Bean was about 41. The following July, Virginia and her mother filed a complaint stating that Bean had physically assaulted Virginia. The case was dismissed, but Virginia and Roy were never very happy together. Despite their difficulties, they had four children: Little Roy, Laura, Zulema, and Sam.

For 16 years Bean lived in Beanville, going gradually downhill. The $3,000—a great deal of money in those days—seems to have disappeared into the air. He tried a variety of businesses without success. He sold stolen wood, ran a dairy with watered-down milk, sold meat from stolen cattle, ran a rundown store, and hauled goods to Mexico with a dilapidated wagon and half-dead mules. By 1881 Bean was spending most of his time hanging around the Beanville general store, waiting for a free drink. The man who owned the store, Mr. Connor, liked Bean, but Mrs. Connor thought he was a pest. To get rid of him, she offered to buy everything he owned for $900 on the condition that he leave San Antonio.

At this point in his life, Roy Bean was staring failure in the face. He had experienced great adventures in his youth, and he had made plenty of money along the way. But it was gone now. His wife had divorced him, and he was responsible for the children. Bean agreed to Mrs. Connor's terms and took the money. With it he bought a wagon, mules, a tent, a barrel of whiskey, and a good supply of bottled beer. Roy Bean had a plan.

The Southern Pacific Railroad was building a transcontinental railroad in the rough desert west of the Pecos River. The land was wild and brutal, and the men who worked on the railroad were as wild and brutal as the land. There was a saying at the time: No law west of the Pecos. Bean wasn't afraid of rough country or rough men, and he figured the railroad workers would be mighty thirsty after a long day's work. In his late-fifties, when most men are thinking of retirement, Roy Bean left his children with friends and headed west of the Pecos for his date with destiny.

The railroad workers lived in tent towns that made most Wild West towns look civilized by comparison. There wasn't much for the workers to do except drink, gamble, and shoot each other. In the spring of 1882, Bean set up shop in Vinegaroon—the largest and most dangerous of the tent towns—located near the junction of the Pecos and the Rio Grande. A few months later he packed his wagon and moved on to a smaller tent town called Eagle's Nest, located about 20 miles to the west. In a letter to the San Antonio *Express* dated July 25, 1882, Bean announed that he had opened a new saloon "where can be found the best wines, liquors, and cigars . . . "

On the same date, the Texas Rangers—who were similar to what we would call a state police force—brought a man charged with aggravated assault to the new saloon, and Bean acted as an unofficial judge. Eight days later, on August 2, 1882, Bean was appointed justice of the peace for Pecos County. In a little more than a week, Roy Bean, saloon-keeper, became Judge Roy Bean, the Law West of the Pecos.

How did it happen? How did a man like Roy Bean—who had no legal education other than what he learned by being sued and arrested—suddenly become the legal authority for a vast section of the United States? The best answer is that he filled a specific need at a specific time and place.

A month before Bean's appointment, a detachment of Texas Rangers had established headquarters in Eagle's Nest with orders to control the wild tent towns. The Rangers were successful in making arrests, but they needed somewhere to take the criminals for trial. The nearest court was 200 miles away. Captain Oglesby, head of the Ranger detachment, received permission to appoint a local justice of the peace. He chose Roy Bean. In the wild desert west of the Pecos, Bean probably seemed like a solid citizen. He was an older businessman in a country full of gamblers, young railroad workers, and Mexican shepherds—many of whom didn't speak English. Who else was going to do the job?

In September the Ranger moved from Eagle's Nest to Vinegaroon, and Judge Bean moved with them. At first Bean took his duties seriously. He was tough and fair, and he demanded respect. He used common sense rather than knowledge of the law, but he got the job done—right then and there.

One young lawyer threatened to remove his client by the right of *habeas corpus*. When Bean asked what *habeas corpus* meant, the lawyer explained that he could remove his client to another court. Judge Bean didn't like that kind of nonsense, so he threatened to have the lawyer hanged from the ridge pole of his saloon. The Texas Ranger on duty in the court said he'd be glad to do it. The lawyer changed his mind.

Although he was a tough judge, Bean's most famous case involved letting a criminal go free. As the railroad drew closer to completion, there was conflict between the Irish laborers who were laying track from the east and the Chinese laborers who were laying track from the west. One day an Irish laborer was brought before Judge Bean, charged with the murder of a Chinese laborer. Over 200 Irishmen surrounded the courtroom, and Bean knew that the wrong decision could set off a riot. After listening to the facts of the case, he thumbed through his law book and announced, "There are plenty of laws against murder, but I'll be damned if I can find any law against killing a Chinaman."

Today this seems like a mockery of justice. And it was. But at that particular time and in that particular situation, it may have been the most sensible decision. In Bean's logic, the Chinese laborer was already dead, and more Chinese workers would die if he found the Irishman guilty—not to mention that the Irish threatened to boycott Bean's business and wreck his saloon. One of Roy Bean's greatest talents was saving his own skin.

By the end of 1882, Judge Roy Bean and the Texas Rangers had brought law and order to the tent towns west of the Pecos. The work on the railroad was almost over and Vinegaroon was gradually disappearing into the desert. Roy Bean packed up his saloon and returned to Eagle's Nest, where the final section of track was being laid. On January 12, 1883, the track from the east and the track from the west were joined with a silver spike. The railroad boom was over and the last of the tent towns folded.

A few hundred yards down the Rio Grande from the old location of Eagle's Nest, a small permanent town was growing. The Southern Pacific was building a water tank to refuel the steam locomotives, and there was even talk of a train station. Bean decided to settle there and become a part of the growing town. Like the early days in Beanville, he preferred to be a big man in a small town than a small man in a big town.

The only problem with the new town was that there already was a big man. His name was Jesus Torres and he owned all the land.

He also owned a saloon on the north side of the railroad tracks. Bean set up his saloon on the south side of the tracks, on the right-of-way belonging to the Southern Pacific Railroad. The railroad was grateful for his help in cleaning up the tent towns, and they allowed him to "squat" on their land as long as he wanted. Of course this did not make Torres very happy. He and Judge Bean carried on a bitter feud for the next 20 years. In most of their battles, Bean came out ahead.

Around the time that Bean settled in the little town beside the water tank, he fell in love—not with a woman of flesh and blood, but with a picture. The English actress Lillie Langtry—nicknamed the Jersey Lily—was touring America, and her picture was in every newspaper. The moment Bean laid eyes on her he decided that she was the perfect woman. He renamed his saloon in her honor and promptly sentenced a drunk to paint him a sign. The drunk misspelled the name "Jersey Lilly," but Bean never bothered to change it. He had bigger things in mind: On December 8, 1884, the new town was officially named Langtry.

After a lifetime of wandering and searching for a place to call his own, Roy Bean finally found a home. He built a fine new establishment with the saloon/courtroom on one side, a store on the other side, and living quarters in the back. He brought his four children out to live with him, and when he wasn't drinking too much of his own whiskey, he was a good father.

The source of Bean's strength in Langtry was his position as justice of the peace. Unfortunately, he had to win an election every two years. In 1884 he was reelected without opposition. But in 1886 he was defeated by a margin of 25 to 17. Bean refused to give up. He made a private deal in which the new judge resigned and Bean was appointed to a special position created just for him. Ten year later, when his rival Jesus Torres defeated him in an election, Bean continued to try cases on the south side of the tracks while Judge Torres tried them on the north side.

Although it was slowly growing into a real town, Langtry was still the Wild West and dead bodies turned up regularly. As coroner, Judge Bean received five dollars for investigating the cause of death and burying the body. Occasionally Bean fined the dead body to increase his fee. Once he left a dead body in the street because people gathered to look at it and then naturally wandered into the Jersey Lilly for a drink.

Bean made even more money from live bodies. He had an extraordinary ability to fine a criminal exactly what he had in his

*Judge Roy Bean with townspeople in front of the original
Jersey Lilly. The young man with a bicycle to the Judge's
right is his son, Sam. The man with the guns tucked into
his pants is Danny Welch, who helped enforce the decisions
of the court.*
(Arizona Historical Society/Tucson.
Photograph copyrighted by Lippe Studio, Del Rio, Texas)

pocket—no more, no less. One of his favorite tricks was to sell a
man drinks all night and then fine him for being drunk the next
morning. In his early years, Bean sent some fines to the district
authorities. But during most of his career he kept all fines for
himself, claiming "My court is self-sustaining."

Judge Roy Bean

The judge's third source of income—after dead bodies and live criminals—was people in and out of love. As justice of the peace, he was allowed to perform marriages; however, divorces could only be granted by the district court. Judge Bean granted divorces anyway—for a healthy fee. The way he figured it, if he married them in the first place, he had a right to fix his own mistakes.

Stories of Bean and his court were printed in newspapers, first in the Southwest, and then across the country. By the 1890s the Jersey Lilly was a favorite stop for tourists on the Southern Pacific Railroad. The old judge enjoyed his role as celebrity, and he always sat on the porch of his saloon whenever the train pulled into the station. His appearance wasn't impressive: a fat, unwashed old man in a Mexican sombrero and an open vest. But his wit was sharp, and the tourists walked away feeling that they had met a real character out of the Wild West.

The height of Bean's fame occurred on February 21, 1896, when he brought the world heavyweight championship to Langtry. At the time, there was a strong antiboxing movement in the country, and the Texas Rangers were ready to stop the fight before it began. Bean assured the promoter that the fight could take place undisturbed. The ring was set up in the canyon of the Rio Grande, just across the Mexican border. Fans and sportswriters came from all over the world to see the champion Bob Fitzsimmons defeat Peter Maher in one round. For a few short minutes, Langtry was the center of the sporting world.

Two year later, Bean's little empire began to collapse. His youngest son, Sam, shot and killed a man in a quarrel. There were many witnesses, and Sam was clearly guilty. Judge Bean used all his money and power to influence the witnesses. In March 1899 Sam was found not guilty in the district court located at Del Rio. It was a joyful moment, but when Bean returned to Langtry he discovered that the Jersey Lilly had been burned to the ground.

Bean rebuilt his saloon, but it was a small shadow of the former establishment—a single room with a lean-to for the pool table. Tourists still came to see the famous Judge, but he was not the tough, ornery character he had once been. He was almost 80; he had a bad heart, he was overweight, and he drank too much. It was a deadly combination. On March 16, 1903, Judge Roy Bean died in the Jersey Lilly. Papers all over the country carried his obituary.

For almost 20 years, Judge Bean had tried to bring Lillie Langtry—the real Jersey Lily—to Langtry, Texas. The English actress

Judge Bean presiding over the trial of a horsethief on the front porch of the new Jersey Lilly in 1900. The men on horseback to the reader's left are Texas Rangers.
(National Archives)

answered his letters courteously, but her schedule always seemed to be too busy. Finally on January 4, 1904—ten months after Bean's death—Lillie Langtry stepped off her special railroad car and toured the town that bore her name. It was a great occasion with speeches and gifts for the star, including Roy Bean's revolver. In the Jersey Lilly, she cut a deck of cards for good luck. Judge Bean would have liked that.

Looking back from our time, it is difficult to understand the importance of a man like Judge Roy Bean. On the one hand, he was a dishonest judge who used the legal system for his own gain. On the other hand, he was a clown who made a mockery of the system he used. Why did he capture the imagination of the country? What was the appeal of the Law West of the Pecos?

To answer these questions, we must look at three separate aspects of Judge Bean and his legend. The first is his genuine public service. During a few months in 1882, Judge Roy Bean and

110

the Texas Rangers brought law and order to the wild tent towns west of the Pecos River. After the railroad was completed, Bean continued to enforce the law in west Texas. In this aspect he was similar to Wyatt Earp. Both Earp and Bean used the law for their own personal gain, but they chose law and order over crime and chaos. In the Wild West, a little law was better than no law.

The second aspect is Bean's long adventurous life: trading in Mexico, dueling in early California, blockade running during the Civil War, saloon-keeping and dispensing justice west of the Pecos. Bean's life provides a human face to the history of the Southwest. Again, he is similar to Wyatt Earp, whose long life teaches us about "lawing," gambling, and prospecting across the West. Bean's life teaches us about "judging," saloon-keeping, and railroad-building along the Mexican border.

The third aspect of Bean's significance involves something that Earp never had: a sense of humor. In his biography of Judge Roy Bean, C. L. Sonnichsen wrote: "Bean's special contribution was a vein of frontier humor, gamy and crude but genuinely funny." In the tough southwestern desert, far from the sophisticated entertainment of the big cities, Judge Roy Bean provided comic relief. The criminals didn't think he was funny, but everyone else did. A century later we still thank him for the laughter.

Chronology

c. 1825	Roy Bean is born in Mason County, Kentucky
Spring 1848	Leaves Independence, Missouri for the Southwest
April 1852	Escapes from San Diego jail
1862	Arrives San Antonio; begins blockade running
Fall 1866	Moves to Beanville
October 28, 1866	Marries Virginia Chavez
Spring 1882	Begins new life west of the Pecos River
July 25, 1882	Announces the opening of a saloon in Eagle's Nest; tries first case unofficially
August 2, 1882	Is officially appointed justice of the peace for Pecos County
January 12, 1883	Southern Pacific Railroad track is completed near Eagle's Nest
December 8, 1884	The new town is officially named Langtry
February 21, 1896	The world heavyweight championship fight is held across the border from Langtry
March 1899	Sam Bean is acquitted in murder case; old Jersey Lilly is destroyed in fire
March 16, 1903	Roy Bean dies in new Jersey Lilly saloon
January 4, 1904	Lillie Langtry visits Langtry, Texas

Further Reading

Young Adult Books
There are apparently no young adult biographies of Judge Roy Bean.

Adult Books

Lloyd, Everett. *Law West of the Pecos*. Naylor Company, 1967. First published San Antonio, TX, 1935 and 1942. A short book containing Roy Bean anecdotes; written for adults, but the style is simple enough for some younger readers; 106 pp.

Sonnichsen, C. L. *Roy Bean: Law West of the Pecos*. Old Greenwich, CT: Devlin-Adair Company, n.d. First published by the Macmillan Company, New York, 1943. The best full-length biography; written for adults, but clear enough for some younger readers.

Index

Numbers in boldface indicate main headings;
numbers in italics indicate illustrations.

Index

Billy the Kid xv, xvi–xvii, 24, *58*,
    58–70
    birth and childhood 59–60
    chronology 69
    death 66–67
    Pat Garrett and 65–67, 68
    and Hispanic people 60, 63,
        68
    Jesse James and xvi, 24,
        59
    killings by 60, 61, 63, 64,
        66
    in Lincoln County War 60–
        63, 67
    names of 59, 60, 65
    as Robin Hood 68
*Billy the Kid: A Short and
    Violent Life* (Robert M. Utley)
    67
Black Hills (Dakota Territory) 1–
    2, 5, 6–7, 9, 11, 46
Blue Cut (Missouri) 25
Boomtowns *xi*, xiii, xiv. *See also
    Tombstone*
Bosque County (Texas) 89
Bowdre, Charley 65
Boxing 53–54, 109
Bozeman Trail 4, 5
Brady, William 60–62, 65
Brewer, Dick 61
Bridger, Jim 31
Brocius, Curly Bill 48, 52
Buffalo
    William F. Cody and 32–33,
        37
    Wyatt Earp as hunter 46, 55
    Pat Garrett as hunter 65
    Sioux and 2, 3, 9, 10–11, 12
Buffalo Bill—*See Cody,
    William F.*
*Buffalo Bill, the King of the
    Border Men* (Ned Buntline)
    33
Buffalo Bill's Wild West show—
    *See Wild West show, Buffalo
    Bill's*
Bull Owl 5
Buntline, Ned (Edward Judson)
    33–35, *34*, 47
Burns, Walter Noble
    on Billy the Kid 68

Butterfield Stage Line 74

C

Cahill, Windy 60
California xii, 17, 32, 36, 45, 52,
    54, 74, 89, 102, 111
Camp Grant (Arizona) 60
Canada 10, 11, 37, 54
Canadian River (Indian
    Territory) 91, 94, 95
Carlisle Indian School 82
Carson, Kit 31
Carthage (Missouri) 88–89
Carthage Female Academy 88
Carver, Dr. W. F. 36
Cassidy, Butch (and the Wild
    Bunch) 27
Cattle and cattle rustling xiv, 46,
    48, 60, 62–63, 68, 74, 78, 89,
    104
Cavalry xi–xii, 3, 5, *6*, 7–8, 32,
    33, 35
Centralia (Missouri) 18
Chadwell, Bill 23
Chapman, Huston 62, 63
Chappo (son of Geronimo) *79,
    81*
Chee–hash–kish (wife of Geron-
    imo) 74
Cherokee laws and customs 94
Cherokee Nation 90–91, 93, 94
Cheyenne 3, 4, 5, 7, 8, 33, 35
Chicago, 34, 39
Chicago World's Fair—*See
    Columbian Exposition (1893)*
Chihuahua (Apache leader) 80
Chihuahua (Mexico) 101,
    102
Chinese railroad laborers 106
Chisum, John 61, 63
Choctaw Nation 93
Civil War
    Confederate soldiers and
        guerrillas xiii, 18, 19–20,
        21, 23, 26, 27, 87–89, 96,
        103
    Missouri during 18, 20, 27,
        88–89

116

Index

Index

Index

Index

James, Robert Franklin (son of
Frank) 24
James, Zerelda Cole (mother
[Mrs. Reuben Samuel] 17, 22–
23
James, Zerelda "Zee" Mimms
(wife of Jesse) 18, 21, *22*, 24
See also Samuel family
James gang (James/Younger
gang) 20–27
as political issue 21–22, 24–
25
Janos (Mexico) 73
Jersey Lily—*See Langtry, Lillie*
Jersey Lilly (Roy Bean's saloon)
107, *108*, 109, *110*
Juana (mother of Geronimo) 72
Judson, Edward—*See Buntline,
Ned*
Juh 72, 76–78
July, Bill (husband of Belle
Starr) 94–96
Junction City (Kansas) 32

K

Kansas xiv–xv, xvi, 18, 31–33,
46–47, 52, 90
Kansas City Fair 20
Kansas City *Times*
and James gang 19–20
Kansas Pacific Railroad xiv, 32
Kentucky 19, 101
Kerry, Hobbs 23
Killdeer Mountain (Dakota
Territory), Battle of 3
Kimball, George 63
Klondike (Canada) 54

L

Lake, Stuart 54–55
Lamar (Missouri) 45–46
Langtry (Texas) 107–110
Langtry, Lillie (the Jersey Lily)
107, 109–10
Las Vegas (New Mexico) 24, 65,
68
Law enforcement xv, xvi, 21, 44–
45, 46, 48–49, 52, 55, 61. *See*

*also Courts and legal
system*
Lawrence (Kansas) 18
Law West of the Pecos—*See
Bean, Judge Roy: as Law West
of the Pecos*
Leavenworth (Kansas) 32
Liberty (Missouri) 19
Liddil, Dick 25
*Life of Hon. William F. Cody,
The* (W. F. Cody) 35
Lillie, Gordon W. ("Pawnee
Bill") 39
Lincoln (New Mexico) 58–59,
61, 62, 65–66, 68
Five day battle of 62
Lincoln County (New Mexico)
60–61, 63, 65, 67
Lincoln County War 60–63,
67
Little Bighorn, Battle of the 8–
9, 35
Little Bighorn River (Greasy
Grass) 8
Long Branch Saloon (Dodge
City, Kansas) 46
Los Angeles 54, 89, 102
Lousiana Purchase exposition
(1904) 82
Loup River (Nebraska) 34

M

Madison Square Garden 37
Maher, Peter 109
Mahko, Chief (grandfather of
Geronimo) 72
Mail 31–32, 63, 90, 93
Pony Express 31–32, 36,
41
Majors & Russell—*See Russell,
Majors, and Waddell*
Mangas Coloradas 73–75
Marks, L. W. (U.S. Deputy
Marshal) 91
Mason County (Kentucky) 101
Masterson, Bat 46, 48, 52, *53*
Matamoros (Mexico) 103
Maxwell, Pete 66
house of 66, *67*, 68

Index

McCarty, Catherine (mother of Billy the Kid) 59
McCarty, Henry—*See Billy the Kid*
McCarty, Joe (brother of Billy the Kid) 59
McLaughlin, Major James 11–13, 38
McLaury, Frank 48, 50, *51*
McLaury, Tom 48–50, *51*
McSween, Alexander 61–62
Meadows, John
  on Billy the Kid 68
Meagher, Michael 46
Mescalero Indian Reservation (New Mexico) 61–62, 77, 82
Mesilla (New Mexico) 65, 68, 103
Mexican border 72, 77, 80, 109, 111
Mexican War 73
Mexico xiv, 48, 71–74, 76–77, 79, 101–02, 104
  Apaches conflict with 72–73, 74, 76–79
Middleton, John 93, 94
Miles, Colonel (later General) Nelson 9–10, 12, 80–81, 83
Miller and Arlington Wild West Show 40
Miller, Clell 20, 23
Mining and prospecting
  as cause of conflict with Apache xiii, 74
  as cause of conflict with Sioux xiii, 3–4, 6–7, 9, 13
  effect of, on Wild West xiii
  gold xii, xiii–xiv 3–4, 6–7, 9, 13, 17, 46, 54, 55
  silver xiii, 47
Minnesota 3, 23, 26
Mississippi River xii, 37, 45, 101
Missouri (state) 17–19, 21–27, 32, 45–46, 88–89, 101
Missouri River xii, 3, 7
Mix, Tom 54
Mojave Desert 54
Monmouth (Illinois) 45
Montana 2, 4, 7
Morlacchi 34

Mount Vernon Barracks (Alabama) 82
Murrieta, Joaquin 102

N

Naiche 76–77, 80–81, *81*
Nana-tha-thtith (wife of Geronimo) 74
Nashville (Tennessee) 24
Nebraska 2, 32-34, 36
New Mexico 24, 52, 59–63, 65-66, 71-72, 75–76, 82, 101, 103
New Orleans (Louisiana) 101
New York (city) 37, 59
New York *Herald* 35
Newspapers. *See also specific newspapers*
  and Roy Bean 105, 107, 109
  and Billy the Kid 65
  and William F. Cody 33, 35, 36, 40
  and Wyatt Earp 50, 52
  and Geronimo 80, 84
  and James gang 19–21, 24, 25, 27
  and Belle Starr 88, 91–92
  and Wild West myth xii
Nome (Alaska) 54
North Dakota—*See Dakota Territory*
North Platte (Nebraska) 36
Northern Pacific Railroad 5
Northfield (Minnesota) 23–24

O

Oakley, Annie 37, 39
O'Folliard, Tom 62, 63, 65
Oglala Sioux 4
Oglesby, Captain (of Texas Rangers) 105
O.K. Corral 44, 50
  gunfight at—*See Earp/Clanton shootout*
Oklahoma 82. *See also Indian Territory*
Olinger, Bob 66
Omohundro, Jack—*See Texas Jack*

121

Index

Index

Index

Index

W

Wagons, freight 31, 45, 65, 93, 101, 103–05
Wagon trains 3, 4, 31, 45, 74, 89
Wakan Tanka (Great Spirit of Sioux) 1–2, 12–13
Wallace, Governor Lew (of New Mexico Terr.) 62, 63, 65
War Department 7
Warfare
  Apache style of 72
  artillery 3, 10, 62
  among Plains Indians 2
Warm Springs Reservation 76
Watson, Edgar 95–96
Wells Fargo 47–49
West, Frank 94
West, John 91, 94
Westerns xi–xii, 41, 54
White Oaks (New Mexico) 64, 68
White, Fred 48
Whites, relations between Indians and xii, xv–xvi, 3–7, 9–13, 72, 73–76, 84
Wichita (Kansas) 46
Wild West
  Civil War and xiii
  development of xii–xv
  geographical location of xii
  myth vs. reality xi–xii
  time period of xii–xiii

Wild West show, Buffalo Bill's xvi, 11, 30–31, 36–41, *38*
Wild West Show, Miller and Arlington 40
Williams, Mr. (as pseudonym of Jesse James) 91
Winston (Missouri) 24, 25
Woodson, B. J. (as pseudonym of Frank James) 24
Wounded Knee, Massacre at 12, 38
Wovoka 12
Wyatt Earp: Frontier Marshal (Stuart Lake) 54, 55
Wyoming 2, 7, 40, 45

Y

Yellow Hand (Yellow Hair) 36
Yellowstone River 5, 9
Younger, Bob 20, 23, 26
Younger, Bruce 90
Younger, Cole 20, 23, 24, 26–27, 96
  and Belle Starr 87–88, 89, 90, 91, 96
Younger, Jim 20, 21, 23, 26–27
Younger, John 20, 21
See also James/Younger gang
Youngers' Bend 91, 93–96, *95*
Yukon River (Canada) 54

125